A Way out of No Way

The *American* *South* Series

EDWARD L. AYERS, Editor

A Way out of No Way

CLAIMING FAMILY AND FREEDOM

IN THE NEW SOUTH

Dianne Swann-Wright

UNIVERSITY OF VIRGINIA PRESS

Charlottesville and London

University of Virginia Press
© 2002 by the Rector and Visitors of the University of Virginia
All rights reserved
Printed in the United States of America on acid-free paper
First published 2002

I   3   5   7   9   8   6   4   2

Library of Congress Cataloging-in-Publication Data

Swann-Wright, Dianne, 1950–
   A way out of no way : claiming family and freedom in the new South / Dianne
Swann-Wright
      p. cm. – (The American South series)
Includes bibliographical references (p.) and index.
   ISBN 0-8139-2136-8 (cloth : alk. paper) – ISBN 0-8139-2137-6 (pbk. : alk.
paper)
   1. Slaves–Virginia–Buckingham County–Social conditions. 2. Plantation
owners–Virginia–Buckingham County–Social conditions. 3. Plantation life–
Virginia–Buckingham County. 4. Buckingham County (Va.)–Race relations.
5. African Americans–Virginia–Buckingham County–Biography. 6. Whites–
Virginia–Buckingham County–Biography. 7. Newman family. 8. Trent family.
9. Page family. 10. Carey family. I. Title. II. Series.
   F232.B96 .S83 2002
   305.5′67′09755623–dc21   2002005247

For those who came before me
Especially Vi
and
For those who follow
Especially Ellen

Our God can make a way out of no way. . . .
He can do anything but fail.

–African American folk saying

Contents

Illustrations

Preface

On a cold 1991 autumn day, I drove a car down the back entrance road to the Caryswood Plantation. I could not bring myself to enter by the front road. Perhaps the spirits of my ancestors manned the wheel of the vehicle and made me "mind" the old ways. As I passed the quarters, then the tall thick trees, I stopped several times and waited for the cows and calves to part and let me through to the side back yard. All the fences were down and the cows had their way with the yard, the yard that had been off limits to their kind, decades before.

The ice house that I parked near was finding its way into the ground, but the wooden gate outside the back door still jingled my arrival. The dinner bell hung firmly in a magnolia tree taller than the house. The same rough rope hung from its inside, still and steady. The kitchen was the same. The picture of my grandmother, "Bar" to everyone who had known her in that house, and Mrs. Mary Wade Woodson to everyone who had known her outside it, still hung a little lopsided on the wall. It had been painted by someone whom my Grandma Mary had raised long ago, at the same time she raised her own ten children, alone, after having been widowed in 1932.

Even though I had never lived in this house, it was as much like home to me as any place I had ever lived. Maybe I felt this way because my people, the ones who came before me, the ones who had my blood, had all lived here for generations, even though a part of the time they had been held and not allowed to leave–or to eat at the dinner table I stood next to.

I would talk to the person who now had power of attorney. He would give me permission to borrow and use anything we found that might be of interest to me or my studies, my research. We stepped into the family's long and narrow library that runs across the front of the house. I knew in my heart that those who came before me didn't come here to read but to dust, polish, and clean.

The books were still there just as I remembered them, standing solemn and straight, waiting to be approached. I spoke in whispers, understanding the sacredness of this place. One by one I touched the spines and gently opened front covers. Mildew and dust met my nose and eyes. I wanted all that these books had, good and bad.

The journals, ledgers, and diaries did not easily give up their secrets. Each seemed like a riddle, waiting patiently to be solved after much study and more thought. They had stories to tell if I was wise enough to comprehend the meaning and direction of it all. If I expected, and I did, to find neat clear-cut answers, the kind that Alex Haley wrote about, I would not find them. There was a Bible with neatly written names and long-ago dates, but they were all the names of the white people and the dates belonged to them. I was looking for people named Uncle Lewis and Aunt Sarah, my folks. I found them in the work and account books. They had been placed there because they represented labor and wealth which equaled power and comfort. They had been tickets, and those books were the stubs.

As I drove off with the books, the car began to rattle. Had I driven over something other than cow dung and dislodged the muffler in some way? All the way to Charlottesville, the car shook and acted strange. As I approached Afton Mountain, the car hesitated again and again. I said, "Don't worry, my dear books. I am your friend. I was with you when you were written. You tell my story. I am Bar's granddaughter and Janie Swann's granddaughter and Matt Wade's great-granddaughter. I have come to save you from the dust and damp and sun."

The rattle and then the hesitation stopped. I drove on.

Acknowledgments

This book and I stand on the shoulders of many who worked hard and had faith, especially my parents. It was my father's riddle, "you are just like who you are," that challenged me to learn about those from whom I came. My mother's "there's no such word as 'can't'" disallowed failure. I thank them, and wish that I could see their faces as this becomes a book.

I have always loved classrooms, libraries, and archives, and with good reason. Generous people can most often be found in these places reaching out to wipe away uncertainty and create clarity. Edward Ayers is a champion at doing these very things. As an advisor, mentor, and friend, he is, I believe, unequaled. Others who read this manuscript in whole and in part deserve and get my thanks here. I thank them—Cindy Aron, Reginald Butler, Charles Perdue and Nancy Martin-Perdue, Deborah McDowell, Paul Gaston, and Alon Confino—for so generously giving of their time and their insights and, most of all, for their interest in me and my work. National Archive, Buckingham Courthouse, Cumberland Courthouse, Library of Virginia and University of Virginia Alderman Library staffs assisted me in numerous ways. They answered questions, offered suggestions, retrieved and placed knowledge into my hands. They helped me get at history.

This book could not have become what it is without the support of those in my academic and professional life. Eastern Mennonite University's Lee Snyder and Patricia Helton allowed time for me to study, research, and write, as did Daniel Jordan of the Thomas Jefferson Foundation (Monticello). University of Virginia and Commonwealth of Virginia graduate fellowships provided funds for me to do the same. As I eased each chapter of this study into the world, Elizabeth Stovall and Kathleen Miller made the Corcoran Department of History of the University of Virginia a welcome place. Work-study students Laura Brubaker, Benjamin Stevens, Jennifer Carlson, and Johnsie Burke Johnson assisted me in wonderful, patient ways as they earned their own degrees. My assistant Patricia Graybill gave many hours to this document, and she gave them with good cheer and the most kind cooperation. And Cinder Stanton, my Getting Word colleague and friend, spent hours in front of her computer working with me to create the family trees located in the Appendix. Early on, she read chapters and never failed to offer wisdom and encouragement. Copy editor Kathryn Krug went beyond the call. I thank her and all of the folks at the University of Virginia Press very much.

Wonderful friends have encouraged me in ways I only begin to know. Linda Alley, Walter and Janet Cox, Terence Cooper, Roy L. Foots, Louis E. Fry, Jr., Beverly Gray, Nathaniel K. Gibbs, Dorothy Redford, Eva Slezak, Jacqueline B. Walker, and Robert C. Watson are some but not all of these folks. My family has continued to encircle me with love and care. My sisters Marion, Eleanor, and Georgia, and my brother Anthony, as well as my dear daughter Ellen–a bright light–make up a portion of "my people." Uncles, aunts, nieces, nephews, and cousins cannot be left out because they have always included me. With all of this said, my sister Georgia has earned her own sentences. She is in each chapter of this book, and on most every page. She searched out documents, listened with me during interviews, followed and led me through woods to deserted places and times, and remembered what I always seemed to forget.

I have unlimited appreciation for those who let me listen–those who are still on this side such as my aunts Ethel and Pearl, and those who are now on the other side, especially Miss Page and my Grandmother Mary. The folks who let me into their homes and their lives were patient, giving, and kind. They wanted me to get it all down and to get it right. I have tried to do just that.

A Way out of No Way

Introduction

✿ Land and the work it demanded tied people together in antebellum America. Alexander Trent, and those of his ancestors born on this side of the Atlantic, started life in the Chesapeake Tidewater and moved west, settling in the Virginia Piedmont to farm rich and often too rocky fields within sight of Willis Mountain to the southeast and the Blue Ridge to the west.

Jerry and Phibbie Wade, pictured below with their son Matthew, farmed many of those fields for Trent and his family. They also "toted water," "minded children," and cleared the straight and tall timber to make meadows for livestock and homes for themselves.

Theirs was an antebellum community, which did not disband after the Civil War–it kept together for generations, even until today. Their lives, and those of their descendants, are testaments to the shared spaces, time, and events, but from different sides of the color line.

Forevers

On a February day in 1787, shortly before he died, Archibald Cary considered what would become of what he owned as he wrote his last will and testament. For a man who held title to over four thousand acres of land and two hundred human beings, his was not an easy task. He appears to have gone down a list of his children, their spouses, and their offspring, first matching his family members with landed property and then matching his family members with slaves he owned and could transfer in the same way. After willing a piece of property to one of his descendants, he attached the phrase "and his heirs forever," declaring how long he intended his actions to remain in effect. When passing on a female slave, Cary consistently included another term, "with all her future increase

Alexander Trent, c. 1850

forever," again making clear his desire in each instance to have the slave children's status follow their mother's condition.[1]

Archibald Cary's will was not unusual. I was struck by it because the slaves he listed, I believe, are my ancestors, and the offspring he mentioned would have included me–being passed on as someone's property, forever. If this concept of forever ownership shook me, must not it have shaken those of earlier generations closer in time to him and others like him than I would ever be? Were there ways to find out what happened to my family–to uncover their history–and to know

Jerry and Phibbie Wade with son Matthew, c. 1870

about their lives and their feelings? Since manuscript census records listed only one of my ancestors who could read or write before 1900, I did not become discouraged when there were no written accounts of their lives or experiences. I surmised, and hoped, that unwritten stories passed from generation to generation might provide the answers I sought.

I conducted and recorded oral history interviews, and listened to each one over and over again, refusing to believe that they did not offer concrete dates and chronologies for my ancestors who lived out their lives as enslaved people and then as freed men and women. From early childhood, I had heard one story and then another. I thought them to be tips of an iceberg, or pieces of gold lying near the surface of several memories, small nuggets of what was to come. They were, but I was not insightful enough at the time to recognize their value. Not knowing the treasure chest I had, I turned back to the documents, including the ones I had spoken to in the car.

Courthouses, archives, and libraries offered documents with names of people who owned land, wealth, and personal property. For them I could create, and had created, family trees which went back to what seemed to be forever.[2] But for the blacks who slept in the corners of their bed chambers, or in the corners of their yards, or in cabins clustered on their land, a surname was almost as rare as an antebellum story. Is it possible to know about people not traceable over time? The slave names and descriptions provided in the written record told me that blacks were passed from older to younger generations more frequently and in greater numbers than furniture. But they were also kept together in family groups, which was a good thing. Setting out to make sense of it all, I started with what I knew.

Three plantations in Buckingham County, Virginia–Union Hill, Caryswood, and Belmont–had been home to my maternal and paternal enslaved ancestors for generations. The family stories, the teaching stories, passed from generation to generation and on to me, were based on this fact. We were from this place.

The plantations in this Piedmont Virginia community had been home to us for generations, but all of us did not start out here. Some of us had come to this place on boats. My great-great-grandmother Juda Ann Monroe Swann said that when she was a baby she had been brought here from the "Old Country," hidden in her mother's apron. She said that her mother told her not to cry and she did not.

When the Civil War ended, my ancestors lived on property owned by Carys, Pages, Randolphs, and Trents. These were the "rich white people" who transformed themselves from antebellum slaveholders to leaders and employers in the New South. They traced their ancestry back to an Englishman, Miles Cary, the first white man to own their land and, I believe, my ancestors in this country. Secondary sources told me quite a lot about him, but much more about his great-grandson Archibald Cary, who inherited his father's property and re-distributed his wealth to family members who came to live, work, and hold slaves at plantation quarters which would become Union Hill, Caryswood, and Belmont.

According to my family's oral history, it had been a Page who after Appomattox had stood in the Caryswood Plantation front yard, barely thirty miles from the last battlefield, and informed the men, women, and children his family had enslaved for their lifetimes, that they were now free and could leave if they chose to do so. "Old Master Page" said that the war was over and that the North had won. Because he was such a generous man, all of them could keep the clothes on their backs (but nothing else). He would also provide each family with a cast-iron pot. Everything else belonged to him; by right he owned it all. Those who wanted to stay could continue as they had before, doing the same kind of chores. They could live in the same cabins. He would pay them for their labors, but he would also have to charge them for what they ate and where they stayed. The choice was up to them. They chose to stay.

With these two stories in mind, stories I had heard time and time again, one from one of my father's younger sisters, and the other from my mother's oldest brother, I considered the following two vignettes which occurred sixty-one years apart in northeast Buckingham County, Virginia, part of the Upper South.

In 1867, two years after witnessing the Battle of Sailor Creek, and one year after listing over a thousand dollars of uncollectable debts owed him by Confederate soldiers and their families, James Moore Newman sat at a table piled high with money. Like most Southerners, he had suffered significant financial losses as a result of the Civil War; unlike many others, his losses had not ruined him. Next to the money, Newman placed an open-bladed knife, a leather notebook, and an ink pen. Using the penknife, he made a "small prick immediately in front of the eyeball and under the nose and the same kind of prick or dent in the center of the U and D in the word United" on each coin. He intended to mark and hold on to everything he considered his from this point on in his life, and he did.[3]

And in 1928, sixty-year-old Polly Wade lay dying, surrounded by family in her tiny cabin. She asked them to give her a few crackers to eat so she wouldn't die hungry. She had been born in 1868 to parents who had formerly been enslaved, and her days had too often been marked by keen hunger. She tried to eat just one more time, to make up for all the times she had not been able to eat when she wanted to, and she died with her mouth full.[4]

In This Place

What follows is what happened over the sixty-five years following the Civil War in an Upper South community, headed by men similar to and including James Newman, and worked by people like Polly Wade and her family. This book discusses how white landowners learned to compensate freed persons for their labor and how the emancipated learned to be free. It is about how white landowners and black laborers came together in work and kept apart at other times. Most significantly, this book examines what happened in one community, using terms that the inhabitants would understand.[5] It is about their work and their worries, their leisure and their lies, their desires and purchases. It is a story of what happened when forever came to an end.

Like all histories this work falls within a defined frame of time. The end of the Civil War provides a logical starting point, if an artificial one. The families highlighted here had lived together for generations. The sixty-five years emphasized here, however, are long enough to tell the story. It is long enough to let couples, young at antebellum's end, have children and raise them. And it is long enough to allow those children to do the same. It is long enough to let ways develop: ways of work, ways of taking care of one another, ways of getting land and making homes—ways of life. It is long enough to see what a new century would bring.

While this long enough officially stops at 1930, lives continued, as the biography of one woman shows in chapter 6. This portion of time is long enough to mark the time when life changed in this place forever—when white and black folks started leaving for more than just a day or so. Higher education, office and schoolteacher work drew away white Pages, Trents, and Randolphs. Domestic work in Richmond took black women. And a Baltimore, Maryland, steel plant took young black men and the wives they came back to get. This long enough is long enough to see what happened after blacks got to be free and to see what white folks did about it.

This book explores individual actions and the consequences of those actions to reveal how people made their own history. It shows how folks often adjusted their behaviors to the realities shaped by others. It argues against simple explanations by lifting up covers of generalities which so often often hide what actually took place. It casts aside the fables that sharecropping was always the same and that whites with land were always successful. It talks about how folks did not all get land the same way, and how some got no land at all. It explores what African Americans' skin color might have meant to their treatment and the names they were called.

This study recognizes a community as a geographic location, in this case an area of approximately five square miles, where inhabitants are neighbors who share work and worship experiences (see map).[6] In 1880, a total of 155 persons made up this community, coming from 38 families, 6 white and 32 black. The total number of persons who resided in Buckingham County equaled 15,540 (see table 1). Out of this number there were more blacks than whites, few of either race born out of the state, and fewer still born out of the country.[7] In this community you either worked for yourself, as did three white families and one black family, or you worked for the Newmans of Belmont, the Trents and Pages of Bell Branch and Union Hill, or the Pages of Caryswood. Church-going blacks attended either Chief Cornerstone or Baptist Union. White churchgoers worshiped at Brown's Chapel or Cedar Baptist in the neighborhood, or Cedar Baptist's parent church, Buckingham Baptist, a wagon ride away.

Sources

This book draws on private family papers not previously used to document the Southern postwar experience, on public documents, and on family oral histories which functioned as parables to educate and entertain. The James Moore Newman Papers, the Edward Trent Page Papers, the Cary Family Papers, and the Trent Family Papers reveal events, circumstances, and relationships thought lost to time. James Newman, Edward Page, and their families headed the plantations my

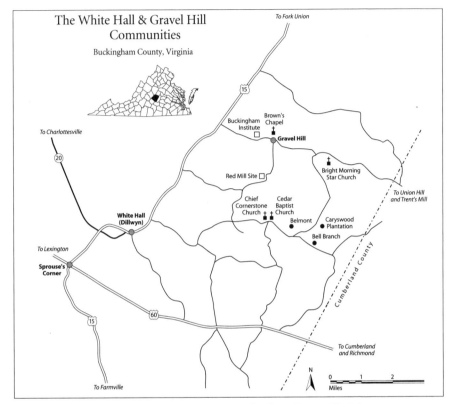

The White Hall & Gravel Hill
Communities

Buckingham County, Virginia

To Fork Union

To Charlottesville

To Lexington

To Farmville

Buckingham Institute

Brown's Chapel

Gravel Hill

Red Mill Site

Bright Morning Star Church

Chief Cornerstone Church

Cedar Baptist Church

Belmont

Caryswood Plantation

Bell Branch

White Hall (Dillwyn)

Sprouse's Corner

To Union Hill and Trent's Mill

Cumberland County

To Cumberland and Richmond

N

Miles

Page-Cary plantation community, Buckingham County, Virginia

ancestors considered leaving, but did not, after the Civil War. The family histories were not chronologies. Their characters wandered in a time recalled as "long ago" and "way long before you were ever thought of."

The James Moore Newman papers consist of five different types of civil and personal documents. Newman kept journals and diaries detailing his travels and other events in his personal life for more than forty-five years (1853–1900). His earliest volumes include an Evergreen Store Ledger and a leather pocket notebook in which he records transactions that took place while he was a store clerk, pharmacist, and mercantile business owner in a town close to Appomat-

Table 1. Population by Race for Buckingham and Cumberland Counties, Virginia

	Buckingham County		Cumberland County	
	White	*Colored*	*White*	*Colored*
1860	6,041	9,171	2,946	7,015
1870	5,660	7,711	2,709	5,433
1880	6,767	8,773	3,123	7,417

Source: U.S. Bureau of the Census, *Compendium of the Tenth Census,* Table 23, Population by Race and Counties, p. 376 (Washington, D.C., 1885).

tox Courthouse, Virginia. In this leather pocket notebook he made the first entries around the beginning of the Civil War. He cites debts he is doubtful that he will be able to collect, addresses of places to which he has traveled and wanted to travel. He even measured the distances between West Virginia, Virginia, and Maryland towns on the Baltimore and Ohio railroad line. The last dated entry in this volume was written in 1867, two years following the end of the Civil War and a year before he married and settled into a life as a Virginia planter.

In a second leather pocket notebook he made a first entry on October 13, 1866, ten days after his forty-third birthday. This volume includes many notes to himself, addressing the challenges of the postwar South as well as his own comfort and satisfactions. He lists recipes for curing cholera, Richmond and Baltimore store information, restaurant locations in both those towns and others as well, and the amounts of cash he had on hand that he took to various places. He wrote the last entry in this volume in March 1870.

A third leather pocket notebook has mostly worker account information, many pasted-over pages, lists of shop work needing to be done, records of tobacco stripped, memorandums of cash paid out, and lists of workers, in which he noted the skin color of the workers he had met and would go on to employ. Most of these entries are undated but appear to have been recorded in the late 1870s and early 1880s.

The fourth leather pocket notebook is the thinnest and has 1890s dates in it. It appears as if this is the small book he kept in his pocket during the last years of his life. There are blacksmith accounts and merchant accounts in this notebook.

Three Farm Book journals complete the bound volumes of this collection. One of these is professionally bound with an index and the other two were sewn together with a heavy thick white thread. Newman himself identifies the bound journal as "James M. Newman Worker Account Book/Expense Ledger: Third Farm Book." It contains entries made between March 7, 1885, and March 23, 1900.

Each of these farm books is twelve inches long and seven and one-quarter inches wide. When expenditures are listed there are as many as twenty-three to twenty-five of them per page. There are as many as twenty-seven entries in some instances. Newman's handwriting seemed to reflect his emotions. Events in the normal course of a day, which did not rouse his emotions, appear to have been recorded in a steady hand in small uniform letters. When his emotions came to the surface, his writing became larger and more uncontrolled. In each of these volumes Newman includes his daily journal or diary entries, worker account sheets, daily expenditures, and insurance records. He also includes merchant records. Journal entries follow this order: day of the week, date, weather, worker status, visitors to Belmont or places he visited, what he did, and lastly his health or his wife's health.

While Newman was careful to label accounts to identify which worker or merchant he was referencing, he also wrote on the backs of envelopes, in the margins of pages and even between some lines as not to waste any space. These pages are often unnumbered, their order often difficult to discern.

The Edward Trent Page Papers are not as inclusive as James Newman's but cover Buckingham County plantation life during an earlier time period. Page recorded in a plantation account and expense book what happened on Half-Way Branch (renamed Caryswood) Plantation both before and after the Civil War, covering an almost twenty-five-year period, 1854 to 1877. In addition to this, in a leather pocket notebook he lists workers and the wages he advanced them at the beginning of each year. He also included chores to be completed on the farm and accounts with people who did work for him such as blacksmiths. Entries in this notebook date from 1867 to 1877.

The Cary Family Papers and Trent Family Papers contain documents having to do with family relationships. Three family Bibles list marriage, birth, and death information for the Page, Trent, and Gannaway families. Also included are store receipts and personal correspondence from 1863 to 1900.

Oral history interviews conducted as a part of this research provide information which falls into two categories: that which is not available elsewhere, and that which is supported and confirmed by documentary sources. Three descendants of the white slaveholding families and descendants of the community's enslaved community shared knowledge of past community and family occurrences.

The way to this community's "a long time ago," its history, is very much like the "stony road trod" that James Weldon Johnson wrote about in his "Lift Every Voice and Sing."[8] It is not flat or predictable or without challenge. The first length of the road, chapters 1, 2, and 3, is paved by written sources. In the second stretch, chapters 4, 5, and 6 have spoken words–sayings, anecdotes, and stories–as their foundation. When written and oral sources come together, their tensions make for a firmer ground, and understandings. This is especially true when one type of source is not privileged over another. It may appear that the two parts of the road lead to different places. They do not. They are, together, simply the path to places largely ignored by standard documents and accounts, with landscapes known only to those who call them home or "where my people came from."

There is a place in the literature for a study that looks on both sides of the color line and at both genders in the New Upper South. A community study, such as this one, allows a glimpse deep into one group's experience, for the exploration of their lives over time. A study constructed in this way provides examples of much that has been written about in the New South economy and the social environment created by that economy. James Newman and other landowners undergo the same type of metamorphosis Jonathan M. Wiener describes as taking place in the lives of Southern planters in the mid- to late nineteenth-century South. Polly Wade lived in the same poverty C. Vann Woodward says was "a continuous and conscious feature of the Southern experience since the early days of the Civil War." This study spells out what Eric Foner refers to as the "freedom masters had not to be masters after the Civil War." The low wages that Gavin Wright asserts were weighted down by racism, and that, in turn, burdened the entire New South economy, are listed under the names of white and black workers in James Newman's handwriting. The discussion here picks up where Jacqueline Jones's and Gerald Jaynes's studies of the South leave off, by comparing and contrasting specific relationships within one community. And it catches the little slips of paper that Edward Ayers says littered country roads leading to general stores and puts the folded and creased orders for material goods back into the hands of the people who held them.[8]

The presence in recent scholarship of studies which explore the life situations of Americans similar to those discussed here provides a convenient place from which to launch an exploration based on the particulars of a distinct Upper South community following the Civil War. While Hal S. Barron's discussion of New Englanders who were not drawn away from their hometowns appears on the surface to provide a framework for Belmont and Caryswood workers, its absence of race as a variable limits the comparisons that can be made. It does suggest why some decided to stay and others to leave. Leon Litwack's *Trouble in Mind* looks at the responses of individual workers to the events that encircled them and threatened to strangle them. He argues the same notions offered in this study, but from a different, more public, perspective. This book's perspective is that of those who worked in the Belmont and Caryswood fields. The sources used here allowed for the workers themselves to answer back in their own voices how they avoided some of the traps of the patronage system and fell into others. Jeffrey R. Kerr-Ritchie's study comes closest to the time and focus of this work. We talk about the same freed people in the tobacco South between 1870 and 1940. These are the folks who planted the dark leaf tobacco that he declared rollercoasted the region's economy.[10]

A Way out of No Way follows the path set by Eric Wolf in *Europe and the People without History*. Wolf honors the experiences of those with privilege and public power as well as those without. He sees all encounters as weaving a common experience, of people moving together toward interdependencies. His is a fitting model for this micro history.[11]

This work, to borrow a phrase from Darrett and Anita Rutman, attempts "to convey via print, a moving picture" of how one small southern community made its way into the twentieth century and stayed there.[12] In order to create this moving picture, as many of the area's inhabitants as possible are given speaking parts. The speaking parts come from a number of different persons and references. Most of the sources are sources in spite of themselves. They come from both sides of the color line, the rich and the poor, and both genders.

Communities such as this one were sprinkled all over the New South. Oftentimes landless whites and blacks living during this era resided in communities untouched by railroad expansion and away from well-boated rivers. There were many workers who never picked cotton but who knew tobacco well. While the experiences of the people who lived in this particular community cannot be equated with those who lived in a city or even with those who lived near one, there were many men, women, and children who would recognize this way of life because it had been their own. They would understand the meaning of residing in a place where the closest good-sized town was hours away by horse-drawn wagon. There were many who did not leave places they had known and lived in before the Civil War. People in this place and in small hamlets all over the New South, stayed home, married their neighbors, raised children, and worked the same land their parents and grandparents had toiled for generations.

What Came Before

On a marble-topped table in the Caryswood Plantation house parlor, there is a stone with the initials M.C. and the date 1671 carved on its underside. The stone looks suspiciously like a thirty-pound cured ham, as if its dusty white color is owing to salt, and its black and brown blotches are tinges of hickory smoke. But it is a stone, and it holds a place of such prominence because its presence attests to this "old Virginia" family's land- and slave-holding status in North America one hundred years before the American Revolution. The initials are those of Miles Cary, a British naval officer who, granted a 38,000-acre land parcel in what was then Henrico County, had it surveyed in 1671.[13] Miles Cary passed 14,000 acres of the land, and the land stone, to his great-grandson, Archibald Cary (1741–1787). Archibald Cary in turn built a plantation quarter and called it Buckingham. Tradition has it that his estate gave Buckingham County its name when the county was formed in 1761.[14]

Cary subdivided his holdings, giving his sister Judith a plantation she and her husband, Col. David Bell, called Belmont, and his daughter Mary and her husband, Major Carter Page, a plantation quarter they called Union Hill. Mary and Carter Page willed Union Hill to their son, John Cary Page, who gave his youngest son, Edward Trent Page, land from the Union Hill tract for Half-Way Branch, later renamed Caryswood Plantation. The last of Edward T. Page's direct descendants, great-granddaughter Mrs. Page Trent Branch, died in 1993. The land stone was one of her most prized possessions.[15]

It was through land transactions such as these that Buckingham and Cumberland counties, once part of the Virginia frontier, developed into early estate communities for the second and third sons and daughters of the Tidewater landed gentry. The Piedmont became a place for them to maintain the style of life to which they had been born and become accustomed. The Carys and Pages had neighbors such as the eager and ambitious Peter Jefferson who married well and moved west with bride, slaves, and enough family money and credit to become a plantation master. These settlers in the Piedmont shared colonial representation in the House of Burgesses and in many cases the revolutionary zeal which evolved against England.[16]

The economic and social history of Buckingham and Cumberland counties from 1800 to 1860 is best understood by reading wills and noting how wealth in the form of land and enslaved persons passed from one generation to the next. While the number of plantations and large farms increased slightly, the variety of surnames of landowners did not. Residents married neighbors and in some cases cousins, once or twice removed.

While there are no firsthand accounts of slave life written by blacks enslaved at Union Hill, Caryswood, or Belmont between 1800 and 1860, oral testimonies and one black-written account exist that provide a flavor of what slave life was like in the region, specifically in the presence of Archibald Cary. Isaac Jefferson, an enslaved person at Monticello, remembered until he was an old man the whippings

Archibald Cary gave him as a child. Jefferson recalled that Cary would beat him with a whip if he did not open the gates leading up to Monticello fast enough to suit Cary.[17] If Cary publicly used violence on a child enslaved by someone other than himself because of the inconvenience of a gate not being opened quickly enough, it can only be imagined what measures Cary exacted against people he considered his own property and with whom he came into contact on a regular basis. A possible indication of Cary's behavior might be found in his ghostly and feared presence more than one hundred years after his death, in the stories told by blacks who lived near or worked at his plantation home, Ampthill. As late as 1919, blacks said that Archibald Cary's "hant" haunted the cellar of his earthly home.[18]

Newspaper advertisements for Buckingham and Cumberland runaway slaves confirm that physical as well as emotional turmoil led to many being discontented in their captivity.[19] Runaways were identified by branded marks or scars, most likely results of beatings. Some were believed to have run away to unite with family members from whom they had been forcibly separated. Church records suggest tensions present when enslaved Christians worshipped with whites. Three years after the Civil War ended, two black deacons were expelled from the predominately white Buckingham Baptist Church membership for administering "at an arbor the sacraments of the Lord's Supper to a considerable number of the colored members, contrary to the same usages thereof."[20] Local laws reflected race-specific restrictions applicable to blacks wishing to engage in businesses headed by themselves. Blacks desiring to raise vegetables and sell them to the public had to have a special license to do so in Cumberland County, where Union Hill was located. The $25.00 cost of the license often proved prohibitive, hence eliminating their entry in this area of business enterprise.[21]

According to the 1850 federal census, most plantations in the Union Hill and Belmont area held between twenty and forty slaves. The majority of the enslaved population was held by plantation owners. Each plantation listed multiple slave dwellings. There were sufficient dwellings at each plantation site for family groups of four or five persons to live together. At each plantation several slaves worked as hired hands off the home plantation property. At Union Hill and

Caryswood plantations, overseers held one and two female slaves respectively. Both slave women are listed as residing in the overseer home on plantation property. African Americans residing within this network of plantations had become accustomed to living within a community created and maintained by the labor they provided. They were also accustomed to unequal treatment under the law, which supported their captivity, and the church, which claimed concern for their souls.

This study area fits seamlessly into Buckingham and Cumberland counties, where it appears that nothing of world-changing importance ever took place. World events seem to have washed over the area, not leaving behind evidence in the diaries, account books, and stories that survive. Occurrences as varied as the founding of an institution of higher education for women, the Civil War, and Reconstruction and Nadir politics may have galvanized other environments, but did little to alter the surface appearance of this one.

The building of the Buckingham Female Collegiate Institute, Virginia's first chartered college for women, for example, most probably gave the area's black and white people the idea that it was going to change living styles when it was incorporated in 1833 and opened in 1837. For the 191 enslaved people hired to build the structure, it did alter their experiences for a short spell. Their labor brought them out of the fields and plantation dwellings closer to the outside world as they worked on the school buildings situated on the Richmond to Lynchburg Stage Road Line. When the school closed in 1863, it left little trace.[22]

The Civil War left this area of the Virginia Piedmont a mere shadow of what it had once been. The activities of the war raged through the region in the same way a fever caused by cholera would sicken the bodies of its residents, forever weakening those it did not kill. Just as a body calls upon its most reliable resources to fight off infection, the Confederacy summoned able men, white and black, to support its efforts. Edward T. Page left Caryswood and joined one of the eight companies that Buckingham men formed. Thomas Trent, son-in-law of Belmont owner Theodorick Gannaway, also joined the Confederate forces. Gannaway sent and lost a son, John, as well. Union Hill, Caryswood, and Belmont plantations, like others in Cum-

berland and Buckingham counties, were asked to send black laborers to serve the cause. Tom Cary, an African American man held by
the Gannaways, was sent to Richmond to fortify breastworks. Edward T. Page charged the Confederate government for services Caryswood's blacks provided when they labored on public projects.[23]

After the community sent forth its best healthy young white and
black men, the Confederacy demanded more. Wagons and teams of
horses and mules were hired out and then sold to the government.
This still was not enough. Black and white women at the Seven Islands Plantation, the home of Edward T. Page's wife, Elizabeth Coupland Randolph, tended wounded rebels. Storehouses were emptied
as wheat and meat were at first sold and then given to the Confederacy to feed hungry soldiers.[24]

Even though the Union Hill, Caryswood, and Belmont plantations still stood the day after Appomattox, the personal wealth of their
inhabitants had been weakened by the war's fevers. Bent but not broken, the owners of the three plantations signed amnesty oaths pledg-
ing allegiance to the United States under both Abraham Lincoln and
U.S. Grant.

Whites launched campaigns to lure European immigrants into
Buckingham County in 1875. The *Farmville Mercury,* the closest thing
to a local paper the area knew, commented that the presence of the
immigrants would cause the Buckingham whites to "breathe freer."[25]
The entrance of working-class Welsh men added surnames to the
area's rolls, laborers to its mines and labor yards, and foreign place-
names to its sites, but did not bring the world closer to the area or
draw the residents out of it.

Visitors and potential residents coming to the area would not
have found very much of a town until the 1880s. The first post office
opened in 1881. Carriage maker William Hall and shopkeeper H.
Murray White joined their names together in the late 1880s and called
the clutter of shops which had grown up around their businesses the
town of White Hall. White later opened a lumberyard which provided ties to the railroad and a tobacco warehouse which became the
site of area auctions. No longer did farmers have to travel into Farmville to sell their harvests.[26]

The Seven Islands Academy, in operation from 1892 to 1900, did not add to the landscape or the area's permanent population. No new buildings came into being in connection with it. The plantation home of the mistress of Caryswood, Elizabeth Coupland Randolph, had turned its parlors into classrooms and its bedrooms into a dorm for young boys. Even its James River location did not enable it to thrive for as long as a decade. For James and Anne Eliza Woodson's son Carter, Buckingham County became only a place he would leave. Its slate quarries and gold mines did not hold him as he left them to find work and education in West Virginia. Thus, one of the strongest proponents of black education never returned to teach in the county of his birth.[27]

Competition, the rocky terrain, and lack of financial support from the struggling commercial community prolonged the time it took for the railroad to come to the area. Eighteen years passed from the first meeting to organize interest in the railroad in 1875 to May 31, 1893, when the train actually rolled through the town for the first time.[28]

While no black Caryswood, Belmont, or Union Hill men ran for office, they may have known blacks who did and voted for them at the Red Mills voting site. Two former enslaved men—Caesar Perkins, a minister, and Samuel Bolling, a mechanic—both ran for office and represented the community on the state level, as did Frank Moss, a freedman before the Civil War. By 1902, however, the politics of Virginia and the South settled over the area, reducing the dimensions of black participation and aspirations in government. The words of an elderly black man Henry Scruggs, who shared a surname with several Belmont workers, was used by whites as an example of the unpreparedness of blacks to understand civic responsibility. When asked to define a representative body he said that it was a "body of baptized believers."[29]

Newman, who registered area voters, noted that black and white men spent full days at the polling place at the local mill. In 1885, he boasted that the number of registered Democrats almost matched the number of registered Republicans. Neither Page or Newman refer to events such as the 1883 Danville, Virginia, race riot, or white resentment and resistance to John Mercer Langston's elections to public office in 1884 and 1888. These events would have reflected political tensions and the reasons behind a decade of actions leading up to legal black disenfranchisement at the beginning of the twentieth century.[30]

The town of Dillwyn, which grew out of the village called White Hall, celebrated its one-hundredth birthday in the year 2000. Its half-dozen streets are a testament to its shy involvement with the twentieth century. The railroad station brings goods but not people into the area. Buildings which once housed businesses associated with mining have been taken over by companies which harvest and process timber. While the gold and iron ore mines are deserted, slate and kyanite continue to bring wealth to the few who control them and pay workers to bring them out of the ground. The building where ration stamps were distributed during World War II is a short walk from where the Work Progress Administration had a field cleared and a ball park built a few years before. The photographs which filled local papers and hung on area walls capture white men, women, and children standing together in front of wood frame buildings or Dort and Ford automobiles. None of the names or faces match with Caryswood or Belmont residents except the name on the Trent Store.[31]

Chapter Overviews

This book examines how one community moved into the twentieth century by considering six aspects of its experience: patronage styles, work relationships, land ownership, the buying and selling of things, and values expressed through lore.

Chapter 1 explores patronage styles. While the patronage system has been acknowledged as a necessary evil in the post-Reconstruction South, there have been few studies that have looked at the particulars of the practice. In *Patronage and Poverty,* Crandall Shifflett, for example, considers the consequences of patronage in Piedmont Virginia during these same years, but there it would appear as if most patrons operated in similar ways. This chapter discusses two very different patrons, Edward Trent Page and James Moore Newman, and their different ways of organizing the men and women who worked for them. How antebellum experiences influenced the development and implementation of postwar patronage styles is discussed.

Successful and unsuccessful patrons are compared and contrasted for similarities and differences.

Chapter 2 identifies and probes relationships that existed because of work. Since work occupied a significant portion of the black and white farm laborers' experiences it is a prime site offering keys to understanding their characters and motivations. People–men and women–worked alone, in pairs, with family members, and in groups of, or not of, their own making. Following the premise offered by Timothy Breen and Stephen Innes that human interactions are meaningful on a number of different levels, we can see how each work situation becomes an indication of needs, ideas, hopes, and aspirations perhaps not expressed elsewhere.

Chapter 3 examines how African Americans came to own land in this community. It specifically searches out the ways African Americans set aside havens and homes for themselves and their families. Land transactions recorded in county deed books, tax records, wills, and estate records made this inquiry possible. Oral histories relate how the land purchasers themselves told others they had managed to get their hands on "a little piece of land."

Chapter 4 investigates the buying of things in this community. It discusses buying patterns and economic trends, exploring the differences and implications of black and white residents' purchases. African Americans who worked for Edward T. Page and James M. Newman often purchased items directly from them. At other times, workers requested advances to their wages to buy specific items. Both Newman and Page kept records of these transactions. This chapter uses these transactions to detail the particulars of a black community's buying habits. This investigation is significant because its conclusions challenge assumptions offered elsewhere in the literature.

Chapter 5 offers a collection of this community's African American family lore, analyzing spoken words as evidence of community values and opinions. Oral sources function in the same way as private written correspondence, as sources of ideas, beliefs, and attitudes.

This community's actions and its reactions did not just happen. They were the results and consequences of particular kinds of patronage, work relationships, land ownership, and buying patterns. The lore shaped lives, bending events in special ways. The past embodied itself into people's lives, structuring life experiences. Chapter 6 brings all of these factors together as they manifested themselves in one twentieth-century life. In the context of oral and written sources and evidence gathered in the process of this research, a black descendant's life becomes an illustration of other African American lives elsewhere in the New South.

1. Patronage

Caryswood Plantation master Edward Page and mistress Elizabeth Coupland Nicholas represented the best that the Old South had to offer. They were born to well-off Virginia families; the Civil War ended the promise their birthright had provided. When emancipation took away just about all of their wealth, their way of life went with it.

Edward Trent Page, c. 1854

For them, the days following the Civil War meant a time of adjustment—a regrouping—and opportunities to hold onto what they had been given. For others, such as James Newman, it meant a chance, if he worked himself and others hard enough, to get hold of what his parents could not give him. While no identified images remain of Newman, his handwritten diaries and accounts fill volumes portraying a man who saw the New South as a place where his promise could be fulfilled.

Elizabeth Coupland Nicholas, c. 1854

Upside Down

In 1854, Edward Page turned to the back of his University of Virginia economics notebook, rotated it upside down, and wrote his name in the center of the page. Under his name he centered the name of the plantation he was making ready for his bride-to-be; under the words "Half-Way Branch," he wrote the year. Page's actions reveal much about him and where he saw himself in antebellum Piedmont Virginia. The frugality which prompted him to use the remaining pages in the book spoke to his upbringing and the family motto: waste not, want not.[1] The entries in this book would reflect his own personal economics, political and financial; they would also, ironically, stand his life on its head and make everything appear to be backwards or at best turned around. For Page, the descendant of several Virginia founding families and the recipient of a portion of their colonial land grant tracts, starting a plantation of his own represented a new day worthy of a new page. He envisioned a life in which events would center around him and his place, just as the space on the empty page surrounded his handwritten words.

Edward Page had good reason to believe that the world was going to revolve around him. His father, John Cary Page, was one of the largest property holders in Buckingham County and held more African American laborers than all but a few of his neighbors.[2] In a few months, as soon as Page could complete the construction of his house, he would go visit Seven Islands Plantation for the last time as a suitor and bring back one of the Nicholas daughters, Elizabeth, as his bride. Their children would have the blood of Virginia governors and a United States president.[3] He probably expected and certainly hoped that the world would center around them, too.

Ten years after setting his name in the middle of the page, Page set it aside, returning to it infrequently until 1877. Entries in his hand show that he had supplied Half-Way Branch with as many conveniences as his father's money could buy.[4] During the Civil War, entries in someone else's hand recorded what took place while he was away leading the Fourteenth Virginia Confederate Regiment. Half-Way Branch horses were loaned to the "gov.t." A blacksmith, Frank, was hired out to work on breastworks in Richmond. Neither the horses nor the blacksmith were returned.[5]

When Page returned home after Appomattox, one of the first things he did was rename his plantation Caryswood. The reasons which compelled him to change the name are open to speculation. Perhaps in the chaos following the war he wanted his estate name more closely associated with his heritage. The Caryswood name would confirm who and what he was (or at least wanted to be) and signal what he intended to remain: an established Virginia planter, from a long line of the same, an estate gentleman with a home worthy of a famous ancestor's name.

Edward Page would not start another account book until 1867. When he did, he recorded his name, the name of his plantation, and the year in the center of the first page just as he had done thirteen years before. This time, however, he did not use an old college notebook, but selected a volume that could fit into his pocket. This appears necessary because he no longer had an overseer who would come to his office to report on the plantation activities. He now went to the fields himself. The pocket-sized journal with a hard cover could be slipped into a jacket and taken to the fields where he could write down the names of the laborers he now employed. Edward Page was becoming a patron.

A Chance and a Plan

In 1867 Edward Page was writing his name into an account book, and James Moore Newman was removing his name from one. In that year, Newman sold the house and land that he had saved for and purchased on his own. Orphaned at seven, the only thing his parents had left him was an older brother who raised him after they died.[6] He left the hamlet of Evergreen, a stone's throw from Appomattox, to become a gentleman farmer just like Edward Page. He sold all of the goods in his general mercantile shop and turned over the pharmacy and post office to someone else. The only papers he kept had to do with his own hair care. He bought two combs, folded the receipt and kept it with two other slips of paper. One slip listed ingredients for black hair coloring and the other ingredients for the newly marketed Woods hair restoration treatment. To make the potion, Newman wrote that you had only to "take 4 drachms of lac sulfur, 2 drachms of sugar of lead, and 1 pint of rose water and mix." Newman underscored to himself that this treatment "does not dye but simply restores."[7] At forty-five he probably wanted to look as youthful as possible even though he was his future bride's senior by only four years; although she was forty-two and he was forty-six when they married, it was the first marriage for both of them.[8]

Newman would have no estate to name or rename. His birth into a family of real-estate-poor and slave-poor western Virginians had decided that. He did not attend the University of Virginia, or any other college for that matter. The only places his name appeared were the receipts and account books from the store that he co-owned with William Gilliam. As a merchant he had done well, well enough in fact to save $1,500 and win the hand of a woman from a once-well-off Piedmont family. He would start off running the farm for his widowed mother-in-law, taking care of the farm which would one day be his.[9] When James Newman ended his life as a merchant, he would start one with responsibilities more similar to the ones he left behind than he probably knew. He too would become a patron in postwar Piedmont Virginia.

Patronage in Place of Slavery

Patronage had many faces in the postwar South. Because it so swiftly and completely threw freed men and women back into a state of dependency, it is often considered the simple lethal foe of those who did not have capital or the access to it. This chapter discusses how patronage evolved in one community between 1866 and 1885. It shows how one community could be considered reconstructed, redeemed, and redeveloped, yet still have patronage hold everyone in place, unable to move forward into the New South.

The patronage that evolved in the postwar South was not new, just different. A form of capitalism, it had first appeared in America during the 1600s on the New England colonial frontier. Patrons were mediating risk-takers, resourceful and forward-thinking enough to provide leadership, capital, and structure where they did not exist in infant wilderness villages. A patron in the community meant that "everyone was potentially better off" because the patron made employment, investment, and improvements available which would not have been available in his absence.[10]

The South after the Civil War was in need of all of the assistance it could get. Carter G. Woodson observes that the type of assistance patronage provided became "the worst evil from which the South has to suffer."[11] Instead of helping agricultural life and progress, patronage "handicapped" it. While "nominal slavery at least had passed away [patronage caused] the new dependence of poor freedmen upon their former masters to continue the institution in another form."[12]

Crandall Shifflett explains that patronage was linked to racism following the Civil War, binding those without economic power to those who had it. Patrons were hence more than just employers. As the owners of capital, they were able to control production and distribution, thereby rendering the market noncompetitive. A patron was able to claim laborers through the contracts he drove because of the social and political spheres he also controlled.[13] Woodson complained that patrons did not employ labor under this system, they bought it.[14]

If Page and Newman could have responded to the negative associations made with what they did, they may have done so with the same voice as a white Phelps-Stokes researcher, Samuel Bitting, or perhaps even in the public voice of Booker T. Washington. They would have been of the belief that slavery as an economic system had given way well before the Civil War and that black plantation communities existed because blacks were too backwards to be free. Bitting saw no alternative for patronage. For him and others like him, patronage represented the natural ascendancy of whites over blacks in the hierarchy of human relationships. Blacks, enslaved or emancipated, were beneath whites because their natural tendencies made them inferior. Bitting believed that whites were meant to rule over blacks because the savagery of Africa still clung to the blood of African Americans, making them naturally lazy, unable to save or to control their earthly desire toward excess. Booker T. Washington saw slavery as a classroom, with the plantation owner the chief educator and mentor.[15]

There is evidence that both Page and Newman shared Bitting's assessment of blacks. Edward Page's daughter Bessie Coupland Page Trent and granddaughter Elizabeth "Page" Trent Bird tried without success to modify the behavior of at least one African American in their employ. Bessie Page Trent lectured Lewis Morris endlessly concerning his desire to spend his pay on any and every desire. "Miss Page" continued her mother's practice, often commenting to anyone who would listen that Uncle Lewis would "give" his money away as soon as he earned it on the most foolish things imaginable. She said that she had seen him stand in the middle of the road after payday in the 1930s and simply give out money to whoever walked by. A waste and a ruination, she called it. James Newman often scolded black workers for buying things that he considered to be irresponsible and "dumb," such as pocket watches or pocket chains.[16]

The Making of Two Patrons

In the months following the Civil War, landowners all over the South questioned whether or not freed men and women would work and if so under what conditions. The ways landowners sought answers to these two questions had much to do with what they had done before the war and how they envisioned themselves afterwards. Edward Page had a better idea of how his community's African American men, women, and children would work than some other white farmers at the end of the war because he had held many of them in bondage. Page also possessed an added twofold advantage: he had not been an absentee slave owner with large holdings, and he had grown up with his slaves. In 1860, Page owned only twenty-seven slaves and while he did employ an overseer, he could have supervised the workers himself if he had elected to do so. Because his father had been wealthy enough to give him a labor force, Page did not have to buy strangers from other slave owners or traders. The slaves Page held had grown up at Union Hill just as he had.[17] Piedmont slaveholders with the largest holdings did not share this advantage and suffered for lack of it. Robert Hubard inherited a plantation, for example, and owned property about the same size as Caryswood. Like John Cary Page, Hubard's father had financed the establishment of his son's first home. Robert Hubard, however, found himself at the end of the war knowing few of the African Americans his family had held. The Hubard family had owned ninety slaves, most of whom Robert Hubard and his brothers did not know. Their father's overseers had handled field business. Forced to enlist the support of African Americans, Robert Hubard lamented, "I have not been able even with the assistance of Old Davy and two other negroes to hire a boy yet on reasonable terms."[18] During the same month that Hubard wrote this passage, Page was employing as many workers as he needed, because he had persuaded them to remain after informing them of their emancipation. Caryswood hands numbered fifteen in 1867 and twenty-seven in 1868. Page did not need the Freedman's Bureau or the Vagrancy Act to persuade his workers to stay on. His front-yard speech imploring them to stay if they wished, or not, if they chose, had latched Caryswood freedmen into his employ.

Even though Hubard did not enjoy Page's labor-keeping advantage, they both saw themselves as Virginia aristocracy under attack and felt called upon to make the world right for their children. While Caryswood buildings and fields were untouched, Page's family had been ravaged by the war. His wife's home plantation had become a Confederate hospital during the war, with more than a few soldiers dying in its upstairs bedroom wards. His parents, brothers, and cousins lost all of their servants and his cousin, A.C., lost his fortune and his right leg.[19] Edward Page became a patron to get back all that he had lost and to restore a way of life that emancipation had made vanish.

Two days after Christmas 1868, James Newman stood in the Belmont plantation parlor and married Pattie Gannaway. His bride was attended by her sister, Kate Trent, a new mother of several weeks, and given away by her brother-in-law Thomas Trent, who, unlike most of the other men in her family, had outlived the war. Newman did not immediately take over Belmont Plantation and have the title deeded in his name. It appears that Newman, a stranger in this Virginia Piedmont community, would have to prove himself to his mother-in-law and the rest of the family as well.[20]

Thomas William Trent was probably a little suspicious of Newman. He, like most of the white men in Buckingham County, had

fought for the Confederacy, while Newman had just witnessed battles fought around Sailor's Creek close to his store in Appomattox
County. Newman described what he saw of the killing and plunder
in his diary as it happened. Years later he partially pasted over his
wartime entries with a page listing contemporary events that were
more pleasant and that did not detail conflict.[21] As a defeated soldier,
Trent would not have been able to block his memories of the war in
that same way.

Newman's mother-in-law hired him for $150 to oversee Belmont
for one year. This wage was both a compliment and an insult. In a
county where the average monthly earnings did not exceed $8, New-
man was being paid almost twice what a white farm worker earned
and almost three times as much as an African American man.[22] It was
insulting, however, because his brother-in-law had had an entire plantation quarter, Bell Branch, signed over in his name by his father-in-
law, Theodorick Gannaway, upon his marriage into the Gannaway
family. Clearly different rules and attitudes applied when it came to
James Newman.

James Newman had to devise a method to find and keep laborers. Newman went back to what he knew. People worked because
they wanted things–food, clothing, and shelter. Newman most likely
determined that he would get those necessities at a low cost and use
them to lure workers into service for him. Hands could use their labor
as credit and cash with him and since he was the only farmer providing such a service he could sell the necessities and luxuries at his
own price. Whether he understood the term patron or the theory of
patronage, Newman immediately incorporated two principles of successful patronage into his responsibilities: he linked with the outside
world and he stayed more modern than any of the people that he
employed.

In March 1869, Newman strapped a money belt stuffed with $620
around his waist and boarded a boat to Richmond. In two and a half
months, Newman had won the confidence of all three Gannaway
women. He listed in his diary that he had $150 of his wife Pattie's, $75
of his mother-in-law's, and $30 of his sister-in-law's. He deposited all
of the notes at the Lancaster and Lucke Brokerage House. With a
portion of his own savings, he purchased all kinds of goods–so many

in fact that he had to ship them back separately on a freight boat and pay to have wagons transport them from the New Canton landing to his home about ten miles away.[23]

Newman saw the world in Richmond, but it did not hold him. After four days he was back at Belmont, recording the names of workers signing on to do Belmont's spring planting. Each account sheet reflects the unfamiliarity Newman had with the African American community. Not only did he list names but he also listed descriptions to remind himself of who they were or what they did. Since Newman had not purchased, grown up with, or owned any of the African Americans in the community, he, like Robert Hubard, was starting at square one. Next to some workers he wrote "cold" for colored, next to others "yellow man," while others were noted by their free status before the war or whose child or wife they were. (All familial identifiers were referenced in some way to men. Women for example were listed as whose wife or child they were, and children by who their father was or in whose household they lived. The widows were the only women who were called by name and they in turn were considered in terms of whose wife they had been.)

Edward Page was a falling star. Now he had to work directly with the blacks he had before mastered. Newman was a rising one. He now lived in a plantation house with people who were respected in the community and who trusted him. Both men attempted to set workers in orbit around them. The community in which they lived had much to do with how forceful their individual gravity would be.

Patronage could evolve immediately after the Civil War in Buckingham County because that place provided a few limited opportunities in a place where opportunities were scarce. There were no public schools for blacks or whites in the Curdsville census district in which both Caryswood and Belmont were located, and in which most of the workers lived. The nine male private-school teachers taught ninety white students who paid $1,500 in private school tuition. While there was no railroad, a public road was being built, and workers for this were hired only on a daily and weekly basis, depending on the job and the availability of horses, mules, and oxen which were locally leased to provide hauling services and pulling horsepower. In 1870, the Curdsville District of Buckingham County did not have a poorhouse or a prison. If persons did not farm, they could work in the one gold mine or one of the few grist, saw, or sassafras oil mills. These jobs in manufacturing and industry were rare; fewer than fifty persons were employed in all of these establishments combined.[24]

At first glance it might appear that Page and Newman were in the right place at the right time. Theirs was a challenge, however. A successful patron had to do more than just employ—he had to make himself all-encompassing by owning or having access to both the tangible and the intangible. Successful patrons had to have land, machinery, capital, and credit. Successful patrons also had to have the power and willingness to protect those in their service and enough knowledge and skill to manipulate social relationships.

Edward Page owned three times as much land than James Newman controlled, worth four times as much. Both men owned only $100 worth of machinery and had access to limited but adequate horsepower to raise crops in the Virginia Piedmont. Like most Southern postwar landowners they had more land than people to work it. Page had four horses to Newman's three. Newman's four mules outnumbered Page's one. They both had a yoke of oxen.[25]

According to the historian Crandall Shifflett, oxen were more valuable than horses because oxen weighed more, ate less, were less expensive, more powerful, more tractable, and did better in the heat. Horses, however, were better suited for farms using post-1830 farm machinery.[26] Since Page started his plantation in the 1850s, he probably purchased farm tools manufactured in the late 1840s and early 1850s. Newman's records include receipts for new plows and receipts given when older tools were replaced. Even though both men had a yoke of oxen, Newman probably made better use of his since he was working with older tools and hence, older technology. Newman insured the Belmont oxen, Darling and Duke, for $35 apiece. Both animals outlived him.[27]

When the farm account books are compared, it is very clear that these two men controlled the same type of land and had similar tools to work it but went about it in two entirely different ways. The ways they farmed their land were linked to how they treated their workers and hence what types of patrons they became.

Between 1867 and 1877, Edward Page employed more than twice as many workers as James Newman. Fifty-two men and women worked Caryswood's fields while only twenty-one labored at Belmont during that same period. Many of Caryswood's workers could have stayed on Page's place living in the nine slave cabins that had been their homes. Had Newman's workers elected to live at Belmont, they could have stayed in one of the five cabins listed as slave dwellings in the 1860 federal census.[28]

Both Page and Newman paid a competitive wage in keeping with what African Americans were being paid in their neighborhood and the bordering Cumberland County. R. T. Hubard said that it was almost impossible to find a man to work for less than thirty-five cents a day or $8 a month.[29] Samuel Bitting found that in Albemarle County blacks earned between $5 and $8 a month depending on their sex and the type of work charged to do.[30] Page paid $85 a year or more for field work and rewarded tobacco tiers and luggers by the amount of work completed. Jobs were often set aside by gender, with women paid on their father's or brother's account. James Newman hired more workers by the day, paying a starting wage of thirty cents a day for all black males; white males were paid more, usually forty-five cents a day; black women received twenty cents a day for field or house work. While these wages were in keeping with the contemporary market rates, the average family of five needed fifty cents a day to purchase necessities.[31] Most households needed more than one worker to provide basic needs.

A Natural Ascendancy and a Fall

Edward Page started out doing all the right things. He drove good bargains with the African American workers he employed. He did not over- or underpay. He charged for all services, not letting paternalism get in the way of the business relationships he had with workers he had held in slavery. Caryswood workers who had never rented a quarter before the war paid Page $30 a year, more than one-third an adult man's total yearly income, to live on his land and in one of his cabins. He maintained links with the outside world, going to Richmond and Farmville to buy goods, not paying the higher prices charged by local stores closer to his home. His receipts show that he purchased envelopes and pens, indicating that he intended to make or maintain contact with those outside of his home community.

African Americans quickly learned that freedom was not free. They paid for services using the credit that Page provided and that they would have difficulty getting elsewhere because they lacked cash. When Anthony Cooper decided to marry, he went to Page for the one-dollar license fee and the two dollars needed to pay the preacher.[32] Page paid personal property taxes for both white and black workers when the county tax collector came around and he kept the receipts, charging the two or three dollars paid out on their behalf.[33] He advanced workers the funds to buy the shoes, coats, pants, and food they needed at local general stores. When he had corn, wheat, and bacon, he bartered them in exchange for farm chores. Laborers could get medical treatment for themselves, their wives, and children from Page's brother-in-law, Dr. C. H. Harris, who had tended them before the war. Harris exchanged his fee for Page's mutton or money. Page honored loans made between blacks, usually under one dollar, paying back the whole amounts when they came due. While African Americans at Caryswood did not borrow money from whites, loans were often made with members of the opposite sex. Blacks did, however, purchase goods and livestock from whites for sums of as much as twenty dollars.[34]

There were things that Page did not do, however, that caused his failure as a patron. He did not become a local government official or form alliances with any of the same. Page had nothing to do with the spiritual life of the people who worked for him. The Page family attended the only Presbyterian church in the community. When they worshipped, it was with a smaller congregation in a more refined setting than others in their community, especially the Baptists, both black and white. James Newman and all the African American workers were Baptist.

Page did not acknowledge his workers' church attendance or worship services. This may have had been connected with his own attitudes toward church. Page never mentioned attending services or reading the Bible. Unlike the black and white Baptists in the community, he did not have church as the social center of his world.

Page also bent unwritten rules of patronage that weakened his position in the community, affected his clients' abilities to do their work, and set in motion a behavior that would have long-lasting consequences. Page sold whiskey–lots of it–to his African American workers. In 1867, during the peak weeks of spring planting, Page sold over twenty gallons of whiskey to eleven of the fifteen workers at Caryswood. On an average of every four days for two months, Page passed out whiskey by the pint, quart, half-gallon, and gallon. He sold only to men and he sold the most to older men who had first been held by his father and then by him at Caryswood before the war. The men that he sold to were primarily Harrises and Wades. Each purchaser was a man with a family which included children and who had worked for Page the year before. The amounts that each man purchased varied.[35]

Selling alcohol to black workers was not an unheard-of practice. Frederick Douglass in his autobiography described how alcohol had been used to pacify workers at Christmas time when work contracts were being renegotiated or when thoughts turned to the new year. Page's account ledgers show that he also sold whiskey to workers in late December, perhaps engaging in the practice Douglass described. But selling whiskey and so much of it during spring planting time could have had a negative impact on labor relations at Caryswood. Did alcohol impede the work of these farmhands? Were alcohol dependencies set in place and associated with hard work?

Selling alcohol to workers was not the only activity that undermined Page's success as a patron. Page's dealings with three families demonstrates how he frequently put the cart before the horse, weakening his patron position. The Daniel Brown, Nelson Peaks, and Wade families had all been connected to Edward Page before the Civil War. Each of their work account sheets start off with a credit already given for work they had not yet done. Instead of setting up his account books to reflect the worker's indenture to him, Page gave credit before it was due, thereby appearing to owe workers instead of having them owe him. Account sheets also show that workers ended years with credits and often started the new year off with more than one hundred dollars, including the payment for work they had not done. Debit columns were miscalculated, always to the workers' favor.[36]

Doctors' receipts show that workers received care for themselves and their families and that Page did not enter the charges onto their account sheets.[37] Page also paid for large items that workers purchased from third parties and did not charge interest on the account before it was paid off. When Nelson Peaks bought two horses and a cow from John Scruggs, Page's cash and credit secured him the livestock.[38] A shrewd patron would not have allowed a worker to obtain his own team of horses so easily. When James Newman advanced one of his workers the money to buy one ox, who was blind, he kept not only Harris but two of Harris's daughters in the Belmont fields paying for the animal.[39] Instead of buying up secondhand clothes at auctions as Newman did, Page sold Sam Wade and his brothers Van and Gerry new pants, coats, and shoes. Alone, each of these actions may not have taken a toll on Edward Page's financial status or abilities to patron, but together they felled him.

Edward Page turned inward over a ten-year period. In 1869 he, like James Newman, went to Richmond by boat to buy goods. A year later he journeyed only as far as Farmville to stock his cupboards. By 1872 he was keeping receipts only from area stores that charged higher prices for merchandise of the same or lesser quality than he had purchased years before. Page also started mortgaging his crops, taking advances on wheat that was not reaped and wool that had not grown out on the backs of his sheep. There were years when Page appeared to plant only tobacco, investing in a new barn to cure the leaves and not planting enough corn or wheat to feed his workers or family. All of these practices proved to be major mistakes. In 1873 Page declared bankruptcy, listing all of his assets on one sheet of paper.[40]

James Newman's patron career points out that the race is not always won by the strongest or the swiftest. He started out employing fewer workers than Page, but he kept them. Newman stayed steps ahead of his workers by making sure that he always had necessities like food and clothing on hand to pay or trade in exchange for services rendered. Newman read newspapers and farm journals, copying down or clipping out advertisements for new crops, tools, or farm helps that might make him a more successful farmer. On 3 November 1869 he copied this advertisement: "Monitor Corn Husker–do 2 men's work–two samples sent for 60 cents or 4 styles for $1 or nine huskers for $2. Expenses prepaid." A year later on 27 October 1870 he sent for the huskers and used them at Belmont.[41]

He tried all types of crops to improve his harvest and lower costs. An ad for Japanese clover caught his eye because it claimed to be "fine for grazing and improving worn out lands." He ordered enough to sow one acre. Not satisfied with the result, he did not order more. He did order scuppernong grapes which were claimed to grow anywhere and withstand anything. The grapes did well but did not meet their boast. Newman did not reorder them, either. Not only did Newman buy enough guano to fertilize Belmont's fields and sell to his white farm hands, he also tried to make artificial guano himself. Newman did not make guano available to any of his African American hands. He was careful not to share his advantages with those he wanted to control.[42]

Newman remained firmly linked with the outside world through reading and travel. He subscribed to newspapers as far away as Lynchburg and Richmond. He always kept his subscription to the *Gospel Herald* up to date. On buying trips to Richmond, he visited pawnshops and attended auctions, often coming away amazed and fascinated by things that he saw. Even though he did not always buy items made from faraway places, he listed them in his diary and they became part of his frame of reference and how he saw the world. In 1878, for example, Newman recalled that he had seen: "20 stuffed seals, India rubber trees, goldfish bowls with fish formed like sun perch, 4 white Chester hogs from New Hampshire, Brazilian coffee, cotton and tobacco, Portugal cork wood," and a woman from Algeria who was the "prettiest lady that [he] saw selling notions."[43]

More important than rotating his crops or relying on tobacco, as Page did, to make him rich or save the day, Newman treated his peers and his clients differently than Page treated his. It was these differences that enabled Newman as a patron and disabled Page. When Jerry Wade's daughter Mary did too much visiting at night, Newman was glad to see her go.[44] When Daniel Brown listened to "lies told him" concerning the Newmans, there were no efforts to talk him into staying on or coming back to Belmont.[45] Newman included the wording "whatever" and "whatever I want" into most labor contracts, and because he was successful he could set the terms, and he stood by them. Edward Page did not write out the terms of agreements he made with clients.

Edward Page found himself in debt to craftsmen and merchants in the Buckingham County community. His list of 1867 debts included the following:

Jan. 1 By balance due for 1866 to Gibson & Watkins	$257.66
Mar. 1 Draft to W. & Smith 3 months	$287.83
Apr. 1 Draft to Hall & Bro	$81.81
Apr. 3 Draft Geo P. Hening Flo	$216.59
July 1 J.S. West & Co	$290.79

On 20 March 1868, Page owed $14 to Wm. B. McCormick in exchange for repairing a wagon. Page satisfied McCormick's bill ten months later on 15 January 1869. McCormick was more fortunate than the shoemaker who never received the $15.75 he charged Page for nine pairs of shoes made. Because the three hogheads of tobacco Page sold brought in only $319.08, he remained in debt.[46]

Newman, on the other hand, set a system in place to ensure that he did not owe others but that they owed him. The owner of a gray stallion named Telegraph would have been surprised to find out how Newman altered the terms of the breeding agreement he made with Newman. The Belmont Stallion and Colt account sheet states, "May 9th Friday–Put mare (gray) Dolly by single leap with privilege of the season at $7. But she took the horse again on Sat the 17th of May, so I changed the bargain by special arrangement with the groom Samuel Johnson (colored) by putting two mares Dolly (dray) and Bet (bay) to Telegraph for $9 for both."[47]

Instead of paying the two area blacksmiths in cash for their services, Newman bargained to let them sharecrop on Belmont property. He reimbursed James Harris, a local carpenter, with potatoes, vinegar, lamb, and beef. Purchases were kept to a minimum. The most costly item James Newman charged was his wife's $18 coffin.[48]

Carpenter Harris had a unique relationship with James Newman. Harris was the only person to whom Newman recorded that he sold whiskey. In response to notes usually delivered by one of Harris's

helpers, Newman sent half gallons of brandy. Harris worded his requests most humbly saying, "can you please send me a little brandy,
if you can share it. I need it for medical purposes for my sick wife."[49]

Newman did not often do business with other white men of his
social standing. When he did engage in business with other patrons,
his interactions were limited and obligations met quickly. John Trible,
one of Edward Page's brothers-in-law, purchased a sheaf of oats on
6 March 1883, which Newman understood he would "pay soon." Trible paid part of the amount owed on 20 September 1883, before leaving the area and the unpaid balance. Newman went directly to Page
for the sum, since Trible had lived on Page's place. Newman recorded
that, "Mr. Edward T. Page paid me above by my taking a tire tightener that Mr. Trible left there at $5 and it is of but little use to me."[50]
Newman accepted the tightener to close the deal. In instances with
other whites he did not have to settle for something that was use-
less, and he was usually satisfied.

Like Newman, Page knew that illness and death were not
strangers to their community. While Caryswood workers received
quinine and blister pack treatments from a Dr. C. H. Harris,[51] Newman sought out more exotic and cheaper cures. He copied recipes
and testimonials for curing cholera. He kept advertisements lauding
the many benefits of "black draught" and for "Peterson's Mad Stone,"
which supposedly cured a man of his ailments after six treatments.[52]
If he could heal his workers with homemade remedies, new medi-
cines, and a magic stone, there would be no doctor to pay and the
sick and infirm would have to come to him for medical care.

In the End

James Newman was successful because he followed the classical
model of a good patron. The 1880 agricultural census tells the tale.
Even controlling only one-half the number of acres Page controlled,
Newman garnered more farm products and hence more profit. Newman paid out $350 in farm wages and Page only $100. Newman paid
household workers, all women, $146 in yearly wages. If Page paid any
wages for household workers, he did not record them. Newman grew
eighteen acres of corn which yielded 325 bushels while Page planted

thirty acres and only yielded 50 bushels more. Newman planted two acres of tobacco, and Page planted ten. In other words, Newman provided more work opportunities, grew the meal to feed both labor and livestock, and did not speculate on a labor-intensive crop.

An effective patron was more than just a good farmer: he also had to have credit and position in the community. This was necessary because the more services patrons were able to provide their workers, the better. In the Virginia postwar Piedmont, the exchange of material goods involved individuals in various roles. Shifflett terms these individuals suretors, creditors, trustees, and tenants. A suretor is one who guarantees a debt. The trustee is the person who agrees to reclaim goods and resell if it is not paid for by the buyer. The creditor is the person who actually loans the money or provides the credit. The tenant in this case would be a laborer who did not own land or have credit.[53] James Newman was a successful patron because he could serve as suretor, creditor, and trustee to his workers. He had goods, credit, and cash. Page did not.

As the classical patron, Newman had to do more than out-plant and out-lure his competitors; he had to keep workers dependent. The men and women who worked at Belmont did not have an abundance of material goods to show for their labor. Newman provided work that led to there being little difference between what renters and sharecroppers could afford.

The 1870 Agricultural and Production Census shows that men such as Alexander Morris, who rented Belmont property, had little livestock or machinery. Sharecroppers such as Belmont workers Barry Watkins, Sam Wade, and Nelson Peaks usually had more livestock and machinery, but not much more. Both renters and sharecroppers harvested only enough corn and wheat to feed their families. The number of acres planted in tobacco, the "cash" crop, never totaled more than three acres for renters or sharecroppers. It was to Newman's advantage if freed families lived from hand to mouth.

According to Carter G. Woodson, the tenant farmers who worked closest to the landowner were most easily controlled and restricted. Belmont workers had so little to show for their work because James Newman had incorporated the two types of tenancy which produced the most dependent workers. Belmont workers had to use Newman's farm animals because most did not not have their own, and they were required to pay out a set amount Newman determined at the end of the season, no matter what their harvest turned out to be.[54]

There were different kinds of patrons in the Virginia Piedmont following the Civil War. These differences were determined not only by individual background and ambition, but also by a frame of reference to the larger world and a sensitivity to the individual wants and needs of another class and another race of people. A good patron had to keep a distance not only from workers, but from other patrons as well. A good patron could not afford to be dependent on others, black or white. Good patrons did not have questionable behaviors.

Edward Page was a good tobacco planter but he was not a good patron. Unable to curb spending habits developed before the Civil War, he fell victim to the same demons that haunted freed men and women, who had started out in 1865 without a cent or an acre. Creditors plagued and then paralyzed him. It was not possible for Page to be anything except what he had always been, a man with promise but not fulfillment. Being one of the once-richest and best-educated men in the community kept him from mingling with "lesser men" in Baptist churchyards on hot summer evenings, telling lies and making deals. He belonged to one of the finest churches in the community, but membership there, like his ancestry, did not ensure his advantage.

James Newman made himself a patron by keeping his distance, and staying independent from both blacks and whites. He did not have to unlearn old ways but he did have to retool. He just did what patrons did—he supplied, directed, and he controlled.

2. Work Relationships

✿ Caryswood and Belmont plantation freed people and their descendants worked alone and in family groups for what seemed to be always, following the orders of those who owned and controlled the land. Samuel Anderson, whose grandfather and father had worked Caryswood and Belmont fields, did the same in the mid 1920s.

Brothers and sisters, nieces and nephews, descendants of Caryswood slaves, now working for descendants of slaveholding Pages, stood in the Caryswood side yard to have their picture taken during the 1930s.

Work

It was work and the need for people to do work that unsettled a continent and generations of lives. For many who worked "from can't see to can't see," the work day filled their lives. Work shortened childhoods and hastened infirmities as many blamed hard, ongoing labor for early deaths. And it was work that defined human relationships following the Civil War.

In their study of seventeenth-century tidewater Virginia, Timothy Breen and Stephen Innes maintain that relationships among people can be broken down into a series of personal interactions which in themselves embody how people thought and felt about each other. These personal interactions provide understandings of how people actually shaped their worlds, even in situations in which they appeared to have little authority. By taking note of the ways people–in this case, a white patron and black and white laborers–interacted with each other and among themselves, it is possible to determine patterns of agency and relationships that existed because of work.

What follows is a look at what took place between James Newman and black and white workers in his employ, and the actions

Samuel Anderson, c. 1925

Caryswood workers, c. 1935. Left to right: *Lewis Morris, "Sis" Annie Wade, Martha Wade, Matthew Wade, Mary Wade Woodson, and John Wade.*

which took place between the workers themselves. It is an exercise that draws on what is available–work and business account records–to present evidence of what individuals felt and thought about each other and themselves.

James Newman

Much of what happened to James Newsman in his early life determined the kind of patron he would become. By the time he was seven years old, Newman was an orphan and living with an older sibling.[1] Newman did not go west to Oregon as two of his brothers did, nor follow his sister Dolly's example and "do bad and run off."[2] The first thing he did when he came to the Virginia Piedmont was buy good clothes; he then saved to buy a house and land. He never held anyone in bondage, but he did hire a black man named Frank to clean his store and make deliveries. Newman also met the old families of the area and through business and church attendance gained status in their eyes.[3]

Before coming to Belmont, Newman had worked for and with others. Belmont represented an opportunity to settle down and become part of an established plantation community. Even taking this into consideration, Newman might still be labeled backward-looking. In many ways he went in the opposite direction of other southern white men of his generation. Since he had been a merchant, postmaster, pharmacist, and small investor for most of his life, it would have seemed more logical that he would ply these trades in the South as it struggled to rebuild itself. He and his business partner, William Gilliam, had owned a general mercantile store in Evergreen, Virginia, a tiny hamlet near Appomattox Courthouse. If all James Newman wanted was financial and personal independence, he could have bought out Gilliam's interest, hired an assistant, and kept all of the profits for himself. With a railroad passing through Evergreen there was a good chance that it would become one of the 1870s villages being transformed into a thriving town due in large part to railroad expansion.

James Newman, however, saw Belmont Farm as an opportune place to gain upper-class membership that money could not buy in

Redeemed Virginia. Marrying Pattie Gannaway, in line to inherit this 233-acre plantation, caused Newman to carefully weigh his options.[4] The farm was worth $3,000 in 1870, but he held $1,800 in personal wealth himself without any of the encumbrances of landownership. Even though the plantation house had the respected reputation of being the first frame house built in Virginia west of Richmond, it still sat on rocky Piedmont soil stubbornly facing the southeast, away from Richmond to the east and Charlottesville due west.[5]

The land was rich and watered, but its streams and creeks merely teased at going someplace bigger; they only flowed into and out of beds of rock. There were orchards, pastures, and fields, but there were also rocky hills and ditches and stubborn dead tree stumps that demanded acceptance and accommodation. The hares, partridges, squirrels, and turkeys that could be hunted when one tired of stream or pond fish were plentiful, but the problem still remained as to how to get the land's bounty of wheat, vegetables, and lumber to market when there was not a close railroad or convenient river. Newman weighed these facts and reasoned that he wanted to spend the rest of his life on Belmont Farm land.

As the years went by, James Newman must have questioned his decision many times. Each season of the year brought its own unique challenges and troubles. He found that winters meant ice, sleet, lost sows having piglets in the woods, thick layers of leaves needing to be hauled, Christmases with workers who would not work, and always the crippling threat of frostbite. If it was spring, it meant that plant beds had to be burned, the soil furrowed and tilled before seeds could be sowed, and workers found to do all that and more. Summers were hot, either too rainy or not rainy enough, a time to thresh the winter wheat and plant the fall-harvested kind, a time to lay by the corn or weed it and the other vegetables, all the time fighting flies and finding time to go to the Baptist Association. Falls were the harvest, apple cider, hunting times, requiring the least number of "hands." It was only during the fall that Newman appeared to have occasion to stop and take account of himself and his life. Each of his 3 October diary entries on his birthday mention that he, the feeblest and youngest of nine children born in a faraway place, seems to be doing much better than he ever expected that he would.

If Newman expected to be a part of what was considered landed gentry in Buckingham County, he was not disappointed. He kept their ways religiously, both in and out of church. Newman's deceased father-in-law, Theodorick Gannaway, had been one of the founders of the Cedar Baptist Church close to Belmont. Gannaway had been charged by the Buckingham Baptist church to organize Cedar Baptist in this community when the white population in this central part of the county grew. After marrying Pattie, a life-long member of Cedar's congregation, Newman became an active church leader. He served as superintendent of the Sunday School, worked on the search committee for a new pastor, and eventually became a church trustee.

If Cedar's founders had been conservative and comfortable with old ways, Newman kept their traditions. He duly recorded each minister's gospel message and commented on the sermon's delivery. When a visiting preacher, an Elder Garland, preaching a sermon in 1886, wore a robe, Newman admitted that the sermon was passable but described Garland as a "dude in dress who wore too much jewelry" for Newman's liking.[6]

In the community, Newman socialized with others of his race and economic standing. There are numerous instances in 1886, alone, when he mentions attending the funerals and weddings of other whites during the work week, interrupting his work routine. There are two entries which indicate that Newman socialized with white workers outside of the work situation. On an early summer day, 24 June 1888, Newman says that he and his wife sat with Sallie Bryant, the thirteen-year-old daughter of one of his white laborers, on Belmont's front lawn.[7] On another occasion, Newman says that he read a church sermon to the girl's father.[8] He does not refer to doing any such thing with any of his black workers, not even the ones who lived in his home. Even though he worked side by side with African American hands in the field, he did not dine, worship, hunt, or fish with them. He maintained a wide social distance. Nonwork activities were undertaken alone or with a member of his family, church, or race.

Newman's diary does not directly reveal any class or racial prejudices that he may have held. Two events occurred, one in 1886 and the next in the following year, which provided ample opportunity for such sentiments to be expressed. One 1886 entry states:

At Tarwallet 2 Sermons by Rev. Acree and we on to King Adams late–my bay mare, Nannie, got frightened by negroes running out of house near road beyond King's and she ran off through the field–my lines broke–I fell out and Pattie jumped out–hurt her ankle and foot very much badly bruised and hurt in different parts. My left arm-hip and shoulder bruised but a very remarkable escape from death as it was after 8 o'clock night but there was moonshine. Most awful places in road etc. King got us in his house in his carriage by 9 o'clock. Pattie did not sleep any, I with her.[9]

Such a traumatic event, in Newman's opinion caused by "negroes," could have provoked him into saying negative things. Newman recorded none. This, of course, is not to say that he did not verbally complain about the individuals by race, but in his daily diary entries, mentioning the incident for over six weeks, he did not.

The other incident involved an attempted theft. In 1887, it appears that someone who knew Newman, his favorite mare Dolly, and the Belmont farm, tried to drug and then steal the horse. Newman noticed that Dolly seemed sick and slow. A few days later she was missing from her stall. To his relief and pleasure, Newman found Dolly tied up in a deserted shack at a far corner of the farm, near the family graveyard. After finding Dolly, Newman did not try to find the culprit or send for the sheriff. He also did not let any of his workers go or mention the incident again in his diary or account books.[10]

The Workers

Newman made no reference to white workers being of another class than himself or having different values. White persons were identified by family and residential location and were called Mister or Miss in the written documents. This was especially true at the start of their employ with him or in instances when he may have had disagreements with them over work performance or the amount and terms of their pay. A white man, twenty years younger than himself, was referred to as "Mr. Stone of New Canton." In recording this man's work activities, Newman always referred to him either as "Mr. Stone" or as "Stone." Newman never referred to Stone by his first name,

William. White females were listed as "Miss Julia Christian," for example, or simply as "Julia Christian, Pattie's seamstress."

African Americans were referred to as "negroes," "colored," "mulatto," or "yellow men," when recognized by race or color.[11] Newman appeared to have considered the skin color of African American workers, either consciously or unconsciously, as he decided what and how they would be called.

Only two African American men were called by their last names at all times. One of these men, John Lee, had the words "yellow man" beside his name on his account ledger. According to the census, Lee was a black man. Descendants of Lee confirm that he did in fact have a very light-skinned complexion. The other man, James Winn, was one of the two African American landowners in this community and owned his own business. (Newman also used Winn's blacksmithing services.) While Winn's wife, Dolly, and their children are acknowledged as mulatto in the census, it is not clear if Winn had a light or yellow-skinned complexion.

All other black workers were referred to by their first names only, or by whose child or wife they were. Without exception, all of Newman's African American workers identified and described as having medium brown, dark brown, or black skin were called by their first names in Newman's expense books, account ledgers, and diaries. Alexander Morris, for example, a man with adult children, was always called Alexander or Alex. Morris was classified in the census as being black and was described by his descendants as having a dark-skinned complexion. In another instance, Matthew Wade was listed as Matt of Union Hill or simply as Matt. Like both of his parents, Wade had a dark brown complexion.[12]

There were communication problems between Newman and his black and white workers. Each work relationship appeared to start out on clear contractual footing. Newman noted specific agreements in writing, listing the pay for the day, week, or month, and the amount of findings or food rations he was to provide. Seldom were two workers paid the same wage. Pay was dependent on sex, age, work experience with Newman at Belmont, and the number and age of workers included under the contract. Women, for example, who cooked and milked were not paid the same as women who worked seasonally bringing in the harvest or lending a hand after hog butchering. A man with young sons who could help out was paid differently than a man with a family of toddlers. If someone signed on at Belmont and moved their belongings into one of the workers' quarters, they could expect to enter into a sharecropping agreement and receive different pay than someone who lived elsewhere and shared a crop with Newman.

Newman sometimes promised to pay in clothes, teaching, and food, as well as in cash. Alexander Morris, for instance, worked for a secondhand cashimere coat on 23 November 1887.[13] For Willis White, a fourteen-year-old African American youngster, pay would be in clothes or the cloth for clothes and Newman's promise to teach him after his work day ended. Willis White was the only person whom Newman said that he would teach. Newman did not teach the boy, however, excusing himself from the agreement by saying that White was too rascally.[14] The white employees were more likely to be paid in cash than their black counterparts. According to his records, Newman always kept his end of the bargain, but there were still problems.

Certain Newman diary entries predict labor difficulties at Belmont. If Newman cited that someone mentioned having an ailment or a problem and then missed a day or two of work, there is a strong indication that trouble was on the horizon. Newman never appeared to pick up on these clues or, if he did, try to resolve the worker's concern. On 2 March 1887, for example, Lewis Wheeler entered into a contract to work for Newman. After being at Belmont for several days, Wheeler mentioned a jaw ache and did not show up for two days after that. Newman wrote that he has no idea where Wheeler is and speculates that he did not want to work.

> March 5, Sat. Morning. Lewis Wheeler went off home and I have not seen him since.[15]

Three days later, Wheeler's brother Watt came to Newman and said that he was there to replace his brother Lewis, working out the remainder of the contract. Even though this incident demonstrated that the African American brothers took their work responsibilities seriously and upheld their end of the contracted agreement, Newman did not comment on how one brother's word became his brother's bond.

On another occasion, during a very cold spell that Newman describes as "bitter," "snowy," and "wet," a black worker said that he had to leave the farm to have his boots mended. Newman docked him for the time away from work and appeared unbelieving when the man complained of frostbite. Newman deducted the time the man spent warming himself by a fire during the time Newman wanted him to haul ice from the pond.[16]

Whether there were jaw aches or frostbitten hands and feet or not, Newman did not address these or the numerous other problems which his workers faced. His solution was to deduct wages and withhold food rations, which appeared to cause workers to exercise one of the only rights freedom gave, the freedom to walk off.

These incidents between employer and worker indicate that the white patron belonged to a clearly defined world that African Americans were not allowed to enter, even for a short while. Newman used a scale of the African American's physical "blackness" to define how he termed him or her, even within his own mind. He treated blacks and whites differently. He was concerned enough about one white worker's soul that he would read church sermons to him, while ignoring the physical challenges that ached and crippled his black counterpart. The ways that Newman interacted with his African American workers were determined by the color line.

Alexander Morris

The color line determined much of how Newman and his workers interacted, but it did not determine everything. When Alexander Morris, a black, married man with grown children, set in to work for James Newman on 8 January 1887, theirs was not a new acquaintance. Newman had employed Morris's son Wilson for three years, 1883 to 1885. Alexander Morris had been born a slave fifty years before and once freed had fed most of his twelve children with earnings made in area fields and pastures. Morris's wife, Charlotte, was the sister of another Belmont farm worker, Henry Gregory. Newman knew that Morris, like most of the others, lived on another white man's place within walking distance.[17]

Between 8 January 1887 and 28 July 1890, Alexander Morris worked at Belmont eighty-two days. As a farm day laborer, Newman did not contract with him for a set wage. They agreed on a daily wage in 1886 and adjusted it according to the level and challenge of the work. For example, when Morris fed livestock and hauled wood, he earned twenty-five or thirty cents a day. Cutting orchard grass, however, brought twice as much–fifty cents a day. Newman hired Morris to cut and haul wood and ice, shear sheep, gather fruit, help with apple cider making, get rails, plow, plant, work melon and pumpkin hills, stack straw and chaff, and move leaves and manure. Unlike some of his fellow workers, Morris seldom left Belmont before day's end. He stopped work early on only five occasions. Newman, of course, did dock Morris's pay but did not list the reasons for the departures, as he was in the habit of doing when he felt a worker stopped without a good reason.[18]

Alexander Morris seldom took payment for his work in cash. The eighty-two days he worked at Belmont brought him almost two hundred pounds of flour, fifty-three pounds of bacon, five bushels of meal, six pecks of corn seed, and a little salt, lard, butter, and wool. In the spring of 1888, Morris agreed "to work one day or more in every week until" he paid off two "old Buggy wheels and an iron axle." Only on two occasions did he purchase items for himself. During what Newman called a particularly cold spell in November 1887, Morris traded his labor for one of Newman's "nearly new" cashimere coats; and right before the highlight of the 1889 church social season in August, he accepted as payment a pair of cashimere trousers Newman described as "old."[19]

Even though Alexander Morris had four children at home aged sixteen, twelve, eleven, and six, he did not involve any of them in his Belmont work. There is also no mention of his forty-eight-year-old wife. Unlike other workers, Morris never sent his wife or children to Newman to buy items and have them charged to his account. Perhaps this is true because, at fifty years of age, Morris may have had some semblance of financial security. His first seven children were out of his household. At least two of them, Wilson and Martha, were still in the community and raising children of their own. In 1882, for example, Morris sold his newly married son Wilson and daughter-in-law Jennie a calf for $1.50 or six days' work. While Morris did not own land, he was able to own livestock and was able to even sell off a head or two.[20]

Often in only a word or phrase, Newman hinted at his workers' hopes and aspirations. In 1883, Newman said that Wilson Morris did not come to work because he was "attending to his little outside business."[21] Alexander Morris may have considered his work at Belmont "his little outside business"—a way of earning extra money and food to supplement his income and main food supply earned elsewhere.

Alexander Gregory

Newman hired many unmarried black males. Alexander Gregory was one of them. Twenty-five years old in 1888, Gregory had grown up knowing James Newman and knowing about Belmont work. In 1870, before his father, John, became one of the few black landowners in the community, Gregory had lived next to Belmont.[22]

By the time Gregory started working at Belmont, his father was an elderly man; all of his brothers and all but two of his sisters had left home. His brother William had worked for Newman between 1880 and 1884. Being the only working male in his household, Gregory did not sign on to live at Belmont as other unmarried men his age often did. He contracted to work for Newman for three-month periods at a time for $7 or $7.50 a month between 23 January 1885 and 21 December 1886.[23]

Alexander Gregory's work and account ledger was uniquely vague. Newman, who recorded every detail of his workers' activities, provided only a skeleton of Gregory's work over a three-year period. Questions arise as to what Gregory actually accomplished on these days. For example:

> 5 Feb. 1 day grubbing at $7 a month or 27¢ a day.
> March 18–20–3 days work-oats-wood +C.
> March 30 April 4: 6 days–1.80 pay.[24]

Why did Newman not make a note of the work undertaken and completed? Gregory was only one of many farm hands during this period. All of the others had their work recorded in the same task-specific notations. The only hint that Gregory and Newman shared a special work relationship can be found in the fact that Gregory always ended up with a cash balance at the end of the monthly pay period.

Quite often other workers would have to extend their work time or come back to Belmont to complete individual chores to settle out their balances.

Gregory did not charge food and personal items to his work account. His purchases reflected the limited size and adult make-up of his household. Unlike Alexander Morris, Gregory did not have growing children to feed. The youngest person residing with his family was Eliza Gregory, his fifteen-year-old niece. When Gregory came to work at Belmont he left behind his seventy-two-year-old father, John; his mother, Harriet, nine years younger than her husband; an older sister, Judy; and a younger sister, Kate. There was an Eliza living in the household who could have been Judy's daughter. (She was named after one of Alexander's older sisters, not living in the home during this time.)

Gregory added to his household food supply by buying seventy-three pounds of flour, over five bushels of sweet corn, almost ten gallons of molasses, sixty-seven pounds of bacon, eggs, different kinds of seeds for planting, two roosters, and a pint of vinegar. When buying most of the items, Gregory did not request the items directly from Newman. Instead he allowed his sisters and niece to get items from the Belmont storehouse and charge the costs to his account. There is no record that either of Gregory's parents requested food from Newman, purchasing it under their son's name. When Gregory bought heavy items, such as twenty pounds of flour or bacon, bushels of corn, or gallons of molasses, he was more likely to retrieve the items himself. Judy, Kate, and Eliza usually picked up smaller parcels such as one-half-gallon jugs of molasses, smaller amounts of bacon, one-half pounds of strained honey or one-half bushels of corn.[25]

Gregory also made non-foodstuff purchases which in some instances met with Newman's approval and at other times brought forth his criticism. When Gregory bought a sensible pair of plow shoes from the West Brothers store, Newman noted the date and cost of the item and charged them against Gregory's account. The same held true for a purchase which included three pounds of wool and one piece of patterned leather. When, however, Gregory picked out a watch and gold chain, Newman did not hide his disgust. Newman referred to the purchase as a "dumb watch and rolled gold chain."

The times that Newman indicated displeasure with Gregory were few and far between. Unlike several other unmarried young men, Gregory was never referred to as a runabout at night. This could have been true because Gregory never lived on Belmont property and Newman may not have been able to document Gregory's whereabouts after work hours. Considering that Gregory always started his work day on time at six o'clock in the morning and ended it at dusk, it can be assumed that Gregory did not have a very active social life during the work week. During the three years that Gregory worked for Newman he missed only eight and one-half days. Snowstorms, voting and visiting on election days, hunting, and working on the Buckingham County public road were responsible for his not coming to work at Belmont or leaving early.

Belmont was not the only source of Gregory's food and spending money. In addition to working for Newman as a farm hand, Gregory also sharecropped a plot of Belmont land. When there was work available building the public road in Buckingham County, he signed on as a member of the work gang. Gregory did not allow his father's fields to go unattended. He once missed two-thirds of a day of Belmont work when he needed to thrash wheat at his home place. Gregory purchased seed from Newman and planted it on his father's land.

Like his mother and father, Gregory could not read or write. Newman mentions that he "read over account to him Sat night" or that he did not read Gregory the account word for word, but "paid him at night at six o'clock and settled–told him the due amount."[26] If Gregory needed to sign any documents he most probably made a small and firm x, similar to the ones his parents made in the deed book on several occasions at the Buckingham County Courthouse when they purchased land.

Just as Alexander Gregory's behavior was influenced by his father's actions and example in the community, it also mirrored what James Newman did as a young man trying to make his way in the world. Gregory, like Newman, worked hard, saved money, and paid his bills. Newman's observance of the young man's actions may have inspired his silent admiration but not his compliments. Newman did not record any laudatory remarks under Gregory's name.

George Holman

When thirty-three-year-old George Holman signed on to work at Belmont, he had been out of his parent's household and living on his own for over twenty years. As a fifteen-year-old in 1870, Holman lived on the rented property of white farmer Edward Shepherd and worked as a farm laborer.[27] With this much experience behind him, Holman must have been aware that the work agreement he entered into with Newman was not to his advantage. Newman's ledger states:

> 1889. April 22d moved up here with my team and hired himself to me on farm at six dollars per month for balance of 1889. I to furnish him usual rations 3 gals meal + 3 pounds bacon pr. week or ts equal. and I agree to rent him some land and hire him some team to work a few acres in corn—but he to loose on account for time in plowing. He set in to work Friday 26th rainy, $6 per month is 23¢ a day + finding is 10¢ a day is 1.36 a week.[28]

Before the end of his first week in Newman's employ, Holman's fears concerning his family's well-being were confirmed. Belmont would not provide for all or even most of Holman's family needs. Even though Holman had agreed to start working for Newman as soon as he moved onto Belmont property, hard rain kept him inside his two-floored rented dwelling, formerly a slave quarter, for four days of his first work week. Perhaps being in the cabin with his wife Amanda and their small children reminded him how paltry were the findings Newman provided.[29] The ration of cornmeal would only last a family the size of his four days, and the three pounds of bacon only allowed each family member a one and one-half slice portion of meat at breakfast, supper, and dinner.[30] Holman had to purchase additional food on credit in order to feed his family.

Two days after signing on at Belmont, Holman purchased a bushel of early rose potatoes and had the seventy-five-cent cost charged to his work account. The next day, he requested an additional bushel of corn. Newman charged him seventy cents against work he was yet to do. On his eighth day at Belmont, Holman purchased five and one-half pounds of bacon to supplement the three pounds of rations he was due. Seven additional times during May

1889, Holman purchased food to feed his family at a $2.11 cost to himself. Over the same month, Holman lost two days because of rain and three days because he took off and worked in his own fields. He also lost an additional one and one-half days because he went to a fair at Newman's church and enlisted the help of another worker, Jim Langhorn, to help him put in his crops. As a result, Holman had to pay Newman for the time that Langhorn spent away from Belmont work as well as the time he himself lost in Newman's employ.[31]

Holman could have worked in the rain, stayed on the farm instead of going to the Cedar Baptist Church fair, and ordered his fourteen-year-old son Ned to help him work Newman's land. As a freedman, however, Holman knew that he could determine his own work conditions and time away from the fields, enlisting the assistance of others to complete jobs. For Holman, the ability to go to a fair, even one held during the work week, was doubtlessly an expression of freedom more valuable than a day's labor worth twenty-three cents. Holman's most likely pride kept his son out of Newman's fields, working Newman's crops, and motivated him to enlist the help of a fellow worker, one he would have to go into debt to pay. Instead, Holman hired his son Ned out to work for neighboring white landowners. The boy had to work, but his father told him where to work, exercising a power over the youngster that would not have been possible during slavery.[32]

Holman purchased more than food. Between 22 April 1889 and 29 November 1889, he acquired a complete outfit of clothing for himself. He first bought a new pair of shoes at $1.75, then a new shirt and coat vest. For pants, he, like Morris and Gregory, purchased a pair of secondhand pants from James Newman during the month of August. It is not clear if Newman sold these men his own clothing or if he purchased secondhand pants and sold them to his farm hands at their request. All three men appeared to prepare for the black church revivals which took place during the last weeks in August and first week in September by purchasing Sunday clothes, new and used. Holman did not buy any articles of clothing for his wife or children. Newman does not mention that he had any clothing available for children. He did, however, trade women's clothes for work done.[33]

Holman earned his wages by grubbing, plowing, planting corn, shucking corn, and hauling wood. When he left Belmont at the end of six months, Newman gave Holman eleven cents in cash. In going over Holman's account at the end of the year, Newman acknowledged that he made a mistake and overpaid him the eleven cents. Holman moved off Belmont property and did not return the eleven cents.

George Holman's example illustrates how the African American field hand faced human and nonhuman foes, and challenges both seen and unseen. The weather pressed Holman as much as Newman did. The low wages kept him in debt as much as did his own material wants and needs. Without land and a credit line beyond his own labor wage he was trapped in an economic system which demanded much and gave little.

Robert Bryant

Robert Bryant can be considered George Holman's counterpart on the other side of the color line. Neither of the men owned land in 1880 or acknowledged having personal property worth a significant amount of money.[34] The similarities between the two men ended there. Holman lived wherever he could sign on to work. Bryant and his wife Nancy, on the other hand, lived on her father's property. According to Newman, Bryant had a "place" even though he did not himself own it.[35]

James Newman's contract with Robert Bryant was very different from the one he structured for George Holman or any of the other black laborers he hired. The contract states:

> 1887. Robert H. Bryant to J.M. Newman (Time and Team Acct.) no. of days that he worked for me on farm + c The no. of days that my hands + team worked for him, as he is working on my crop by my own crop hands. I to return his work done on my crop by my hands working for him day for day which to this own findings–+ he to work so many days for me to pay for my team–when he uses them for his individual work such as moving his corn +c here +c.[36]

It appears that Bryant did not move his entire family onto Belmont property at first. Saturday, 26 November 1887, Newman recorded that "Bob Bryant moved in some of his things–self and son

Daniel–to work on shares for one year."[37] There is no mention of Nancy Bryant, John's wife, their older son Jim, or their daughter Sallie moving in or staying behind someplace else. Bryant, unlike Holman, had access to a wagon in which to transport his belongings and was not charged.[38]

The first four months Bryant worked for Newman, the ledger indicates that Newman stayed true to the contract, crediting his account for tasks completed in full or half days, not money. In some instances, if Bryant did a particularly hard job and it took only one day, Newman would credit him with as many as three days' pay. The Saturday, 3 December 1887, entry states, "To my team 1 day oxen and cart load corn in from Bob Hubbard's mill."[39] Instead of crediting Bryant with one day's work, he rewarded him with two and one-half days' credit. Nine days later, Newman appeared to be even more generous: "Monday, 12 December 1887–To my horse team and wagon one day to haul corn from Hubbard's mill down here."[40] Bryant received three and one-half days' credit for this single day of work.

Bryant's work ledger seems to indicate that he worked as a skilled and unskilled worker. He must have been able to build and repair structures because he worked on the ice house and constructed a sheep shelter.[41] He assisted Newman when hog butchering time rolled around by doing everything from preparing the big Belmont kettle to hanging up the cut, quartered, and salted carcasses. Bryant put his shoulder to the plow in the spring and threshed, shacked, and harrowed what grew. He cleaned the chicken yard and pulled props from under the barn. All in all, he did much of the same work the black workers did. The only difference was that he worked under different terms and received higher pay.

Newman sent Bryant on errands which would take him farther away than he allowed black workers to go with his teams and wagons. Whereas Alexander Morris did sell melons for Newman at the Buckingham County Courthouse, Newman journeyed with him there and stayed until all the melons were gone. Bryant, four years younger than Morris, traveled alone to the Cumberland County Courthouse and sold melons without Newman's supervision or watchful eye.[42] Black workers took wheat and corn to the two mills closest by, whereas Bryant took the ox team to Hubbard's Mill farther away by miles than either of the others. Bryant was also the only worker to travel alone to Arvonia to truck goods or pick up packages.[43]

When Newman started paying Bryant in cash, he did not use the same pay scale he made available to black workers. While experienced hand Alexander Morris earned twenty-five or thirty cents a day, and the younger, less experienced George Holman, twenty-three cents a day, Bryant earned forty-two cents a day. Jim and Daniel Bryant were paid exactly half of what their father earned most of his time. On more than one occasion, however, especially if they worked less than an entire day, Newman paid them forty-two cents a day, significantly more than any of the African American workers earned.

Just as Bryant's contract, work conditions, and wage rate differed from those of adult black men, so did his purchasing habits. Bryant purchased so much flour–235 pounds–that he may have been buying the flour from Newman and selling it to others at a profit. Unlike black workers, Bryant did not purchase one pound of bacon or one sack of cornmeal. He did buy three pecks of seed from Newman, suggesting an independence he had to plant crops away from Newman and Belmont. Bryant was the only Belmont worker who purchased guano. He bought twelve pounds of it and took two days to spread it over his plant patches before he sowed the seeds he had also purchased.

When Bryant left Belmont, he, like George Holman, owed James Newman money. In Bryant's case, however, he was not in debt to Newman for eleven cents but for $5.26. Like other hands, Bryant pledged his tobacco crop against the unpaid amount. And like other hands, his crop did not meet his expectation. The final entries under Bryant's name tell the tale of his unpleasant parting:

1888–Oct. 15th Balance Due J.M. Newman	$5.26
1889–Mar. 13th By cash in Farmville out of your half of tobacco crop	$3.13
Mar. 14 - Besides hauling tobacco (for) 1.20, Bryant is still due me this	$2.13[44]

Five years later, the bill was still unpaid. A June 1896 entry indicates that Newman took final payment on this account in the form of "1 crippled shoat" worth $2.33. This amount did not satisfy the whole account because Newman had been charging Bryant interest for five years. The last entry that Newman made referring to Bryant was scrawled in a loose undisciplined hand, very uncharacteristic of James Newman. It stated, "I have no use for the gentleman, he let his hogs eat up my wheat lot."[45]

Davy Harris and His Daughters

None of the men, black or white, who worked at Belmont enlisted the labor of their wives in tending Newman's land.[46] One black man, Davy Harris, however, found himself in a financial situation very similar to Robert Bryant's, owing Newman almost a month's wages, with no cash reserve available to pay him back. Having no sons at home, Harris had to consider bringing his daughters with him into the fields to work off his debt. On 6 November 1886, Newman wrote on an empty page in his account book under the heading *Davy Harris:*

> 1886 Nov. 6th–To 1 young bull oxen as per due bill and lien on his present crop of tobacco for payment of $15 and waiving all exemptions.[47]

While the terms of this agreement appear to be straightforward and unthreatening, the term "and waiving all exemptions" must have struck fear in Harris's heart and given Newman an added assurance. To waive all exemptions meant to agree that any and all personal property could be attached for payment of a debt. In other words, when Harris entered into this agreement with Newman, Harris gave up the protection that saved "debtors from total loss, to prevent them from losing everything they had."[48] On the other hand, as the contract was written, Newman was protected by the Virginia General Assembly's 1873 Homestead Exemption Act, which states in part that

> The Lien shall not in any manner affect the rights of landlords to their proper share of rents or right of distress, nor existing liens, nor shall it affect the advancee's rights to claim such part of his crop as is non exempt from levy or distress for rent.[49]

Harris must have breathed a great deal easier when on 11 March 1887, Newman credited his account with $12.00, leaving only an unpaid balance of $3.00 against the purchase of the bull ox. On 2 and 3

May 1887, Harris cut rails and worked in one of Belmont's melon patches to earn money to pay off the balance. He only earned seventy-five cents for two days' labor. At the end of June, Harris returned to Belmont, but this time he was not alone. Both of his daughters, grown unmarried women, accompanied him and spent three days working with him in Newman's fields. Each woman was paid twenty cents per day. The $1.20 that they earned was credited to their father's account, reducing his debt to a manageable $1.05. Harris cut, stacked, and cultivated Belmont wheat until he paid off the final balance.[50]

The two Harris sisters did not immediately return to Belmont to work. When they did, their days' work was once again recorded under their father's name even though for the first time they were paid directly for one day of their work and allowed to spend their wages for the other day at the West Brothers store. The entries state:

> 1887 Oct. 1 By Ella + Fanny 1 day sweet potatoes   50¢.
> Cash pd them full   50¢
> Oct. 18–17th Ella + Fanny 1/2 day = 1 day each pull =
> shuck corn   20¢
> 60¢
> Oct. 31 - To order to West Bro +Co in full above work   60¢[51]

Perhaps it was because of the field hand experiences and the treat of buying things at the West Brothers store that Ella Harris was willing to work for Pattie Newman inside the Belmont home, even if all of her work was still recorded under her father's name. On 2 January 1888, Newman wrote:

> Jan. 2nd. His Daughter Ella set in to cook-wash-milk +c for us this year at $25 per year and her rations. 20 8c per month + some presents if Pattie chooses.[52]

Four days later, Ella started a buying trend that she would maintain her entire time in Newman's employ. On 6 January 1888 she went to West Brothers and purchased a horn comb and a head of cabbage.[53] Almost without exception whenever she purchased an item for her family she also bought something for her own individual use.

During Ella Harris's early months working at Belmont, her father's account ledger spoke of her work and debits just as often as it did of his own. In certain instances, it is difficult to identify which of them did what and for how much. On 24 and 25 January 1888, for example, who helped with the ice-getting and cleaned out the stables and ox stalls?[54] It seems that Davy Harris probably did this type of work, but it is also not out of the question that his daughter, a former field-worker, could have also accomplished the same tasks.

Davy Harris frequently instructed his daughter to bring food items home from Belmont. On 21 March 1888, for example, Ella, at her father's request, bought one dozen eggs from Newman, and had them charged under her father's name to be paid for with work that she herself did.[55] On 9 May 1888, Newman settled the Harris account by sending $6.18 to Davy Harris as payment to him for wages his daughter earned. If Ella received any cash payment for her toil, Newman did not mention it.[56]

Ella Harris shared few of the buying habits of her male African American counterparts. Like them she purchased several kinds of white and sweet potatoes, flour, bacon, chicken, vinegar, and wheat. But she also purchased gifts of food for persons outside her family group. She gave away onion seeds to another black woman, Martha Gregory. She also gave George Holman's wife, Amanda, pounds of butter on different occasions. Most of Ella Harris's earnings, all not turned over to her father, were spent on fabric, ready-made clothing items, and household goods. During the four years that Harris worked for Newman, she purchased the following types of cloth:

15.5 yards checked domestic cotton
15 yards calico
10 yards blue cashmere
7 yards plain domestic cotton
3 yards brown domestic
1/2 yard black velvet[57]

Because Newman did not mention that Harris secured the services of a dressmaker, it can be assumed that she made her own clothes. Further evidence of her clothes-making ability can also be found in the spools of "cotton" she frequently purchased from West Brothers store.[58] Harris also purchased more kerosene oil than any other Belmont worker between 1886 and 1890.[59] She could have used the oil in a chimney lamp she also purchased from Newman to sew by at home, in the evenings after her working hours.

Ella Harris also contributed to her church more often and in greater amounts than any of the men who worked for Newman.[60] Her father's work account sheet shows that Ella went to church throughout the year and regularly requested wage advances so that she could tithe. The average amount of her church offering was twenty-seven cents, which would have equaled a little over one day's work if she, instead of her father, had received her earned wage.

Ella Harris's purchases suggest much about her personality and future plans. She placed nine orders at the West Brothers store, significantly more than the African American males who worked for Newman. Unlike them, she purchased furniture and kitchenware. A set of knives and forks, a clothes trunk, and a chair became hers while she was employed at Belmont. The secondhand white kid leather gloves suggest that she considered herself a lady even though she had spent many days working in the fields. The postage stamp that she purchased indicates that Buckingham County was not her whole world. Whether she could read and write remains unanswered.

Ella Harris's name disappears from the Belmont work ledger in 1890, but she in fact did not leave the area or conclude her relationship with the Newmans and Belmont. Harris married Isaiah "Zee" Ayers, an African American man, who had previously worked at Belmont and who would come back time and again to do so during the 1890s.[61] By December 1891 they were the parents of a son, Walker, and the next year, another son, David, named after Ella's father. Zee and Ella Ayers named one of their daughters Pattie. Pattie Ayers could have been named after Pattie Newman. The act of giving a child the same name as another person, even if the child is not named directly after this person, is significant, indicating a positive bond. Ella Harris Ayers must have had pleasant recollections of her interactions with her employers.

Ella Harris's work at Belmont was characteristic of the female African American work experience in the New South. Like the African American enslaved woman, she worked outside of her household; unlike them she did not do the same types of work as men on a consistent basis. Like other rural African American women, her absence or presence in the work force was dependent on the able-bodied men in her life who could put her into or take her out of the work force at their discretion.[62] Ella Harris's wages were lower than her male counterparts'. Harris earned $25 per year compared to the $85 average amount paid to male African American workers. Belmont workers, male and female, earned significantly less than black rural workers elsewhere. Freedman's Bureau records show that the average wage was $10 to $12 per month for men and $8 per month for women.[63]

Doing unto Others

Even though the Belmont documents recorded the thoughts of only one person, James Newman, the work activities of his records attest to the daily instances when workers earned money to purchase items for others, or to pay off debts that they had made to other African Americans for livestock, food, or cash. These acts of generosity by those who had so few material possessions suggest a tightly woven and caring community.

James Newman's records also point out that persons with the same surnames worked together. The federal censuses of 1870 and 1880 established the relationships between these workers. Combining the evidence of these sources, it is apparent that there were strong nuclear and extended black family networks which survived slavery and the Civil War. The Harris, Gregory, and Morris families were examples of the case in point. Alexander Morris married John Gregory's oldest daughter, Charlotte. Alexander and Charlotte's son, Wilson, would live with one of John Gregory's sons, Henry. Even after his marriage, Wilson Morris continued to demonstrate how important family members were to him. On 7 March 1885 he treated his first cousin Mary Wade to "1 lb. best dried peaches."[64] He also satisfied Wade's debt to Newman when she stopped working for Newman, but still owed money to him because she had been overpaid when she left. Newman wrote:

> April 17th. Tuesday, Mary Wade left and quit cooking, washing +c for us. By 2 months cooking, washing +c for us, but she did not suit

us as she lost time nearly every evening leaving her business and going off to Wilson's home and in the neighborhood and to the Creacys.[65]

Newman paid her $5 but also gave her one barrel of family flour that he forgot to write down on her account. Wilson Morris agreed to pay the cost of the flour out of his wages. The $5 sum represented almost all of Morris's wages for a month.

Three of Wilson Morris's siblings worked at Belmont, as did his wife, father, and son. Seven of John Gregory's eleven children and one of his grandchildren worked for Newman, over a ten-year period.

Not only did Davy Harris work at Belmont, but his daughter Ella also lived there after she married Zee Ayers in 1891. In 1891 there were five members of the Harris family working or living on Belmont property: Davy, his younger daughter Fannie, Ella, her husband Zee Ayers, and their infant, Walker. The work accounts of Davy and Fannie Harris and Zee Ayers illustrate that they charged items to each other's accounts and purchased items that each other used.

Wilson Morris and the Harrises were not alone in their expressions of generosity to family and friends. Belmont Plantation African American workers support the observation made by Jones that states, "Blacks did not work as individuals, they did not go in for materialistic individualism."[66] Workers like Henry Cunningham left Belmont fields for three days to look after a sick sister. He was docked an additional one-half day's pay to attend her funeral.[67]

Not a week passed that a Belmont worker did not purchase a gift of food or clothing and have the cost taken out of their wages. Basic food supplies such as flour and bacon were given to extended family members living out of the gifter's household. Friends and neighbors were also the recipients of food and luxuries such as honey, sugar, and butter.

African American women waited on the sick away from their homes in winter and accepted rides back to their homes when deep snow made walking difficult. Newman deducted the costs for the horse's hire out of each worker's pay. Field hands took time off to attend weddings and funerals and lost wages to do so.

African Americans most often worked in pairs. Newman made no references to conflicts which occurred between workers. He did mention disagreements, but they were all between himself and his workers. Wilson Morris and Alexander Gregory were of the same opinion when they refused to skin an old steer that died in a Belmont meadow.[68] Newman expressed doubt that two of his other workers were actually disposing of another dead animal as he had ordered them to do. He believed that two African American males got together and "pretended to burn" the cow carcass. Newman suspected that the two men were in fact going to keep the beef for themselves.

African American workers borrowed money from each other and repaid it. They purchased hogs and cows and chickens from each other and respected the terms of the bargains they struck. They enlisted each other's help in planting and harvesting crops, even when they had to pay James Newman for the assisting worker's time.

African Americans honored debts that they made with each other, paying back money and food in a timely manner. They also accepted each other's word as truth, several times declining Belmont work, if they had been told what Newman called "lies" about his not being a fair employer. Males in the community often adopted orphan boys and bargained with Newman to get a job and a fair rate of pay. There were strong mother-son relationships, displayed for example by Watt Wheeler who purchased items from Newman specifically for his mother, or others who worked to earn the money to buy items for their mothers from the general store.

Newman knew about interactions between African Americans who worked for him because of his part in providing their work, food, and material goods. His presence may have affected the relationships between blacks in some way. Newman, for example, did not hide his contempt for Wilson Morris. When Morris returned to Belmont for a visit after living and working elsewhere, he discussed the "sprinkling of children" with Newman. Newman wrote that Morris, referring to a child's christening, was talking foolishness and dismissed him and his comments. Similar expressions of differing opinions could have caused Newman to let workers go, thus making them unable to interact with other field hands as they may have wished. When Alexander Morris became angry at Newman and said that he was moving out of the Belmont quarters into a suitable place to "put his daughter's fine things," Newman bid him farewell and vowed never to hire him back. Morris would no longer have access to Belmont wages or the work experiences that came before those wages were paid.

James Newman may not have been an extremely wealthy man, but he was certainly very well off by the standards of his society. His income steadily increased during this period. He was able to invest in bonds, write drafts, pay his land and personal property taxes, subscribe to newspapers, and pay his church subscriptions on time and with ease. The slow pace of economic growth in the South is partly explainable through worker wages that did not increase because men such as Newman held the profits. The Belmont farm experience shows how women were kept out of the work force if their fathers or husbands could get by without them and how they were drawn back into it if they could not.

African Americans and whites treated each other differently. The same men who would vote together and work in the same fields would not eat what they had harvested together at the same table. They would not give gifts to each other, only to members of their own respective races. While men like Newman paid African American workers in secondhand clothes, white workers at Belmont did not accept the hand-me-downs of their employer. It was as if the white workers said, "since we share the same skin color, we will not share the same garments."

Paternalism on the Belmont Farm was often laced with contempt, impatience, and condescension. African Americans' opinions were considered "foolishness" and their purchases "dumb." Their hopes were summarily dismissed with phrases written in bold thick letters. Over and over again, Newman wrote the words, "whatever suits me" and "whatever I say" and "anything I please" into the contracts of his employees. The land he owned and the work he provided allowed him to do so.

3. Land Acquisition

❧ Edward Page's father's money built the Caryswood Plantation House in 1857. A hundred years after its construction, Page's granddaughter's husband spent most of every waking hour picking up the rocks that seemed to sprout up more readily than blades of grass.

Family legend claims that the land actually killed Van Woodson. His profits from two premium dark leaf tobacco crops had bought the home place in the early 1920s and supplied the money to build the dwelling pictured here by 1925. In an effort to clear the land of its many rocks, Woodson over and over again pressed as many boulders as he could against his body as he cleared for the family's home and outhouses. Over time, the skin on Woodson's abdomen wore away, becoming the host of a cancer that bloodied the mountain of rocks he moved from the places he intended for his family and animals.

Caryswood Plantation House, c. 1930

On the last day of August 1874, the former slave John Gregory walked into the Buckingham County, Virginia, courthouse with his wife Harriet and thirty dollars in his pocket. The courthouse was new, the replacement for the original building which had burned down five years before. The old courthouse had held bills of sale for Buckingham County real estate and personal property. A document listing John or Harriet Gregory's name could have been filed in the old courthouse records. If so, it would have identified them as the purchased and not the purchasers of property. But an 1869 fire had destroyed all of the documentation of human bondage, and this new courthouse would hold the proof that this couple, considered material property just ten years before, became property owners themselves, on this late summer day.[1]

When the Gregorys made marks beneath their neatly scripted names on the land deed, legalizing their purchase, their action stood for a remarkable feat. Their x's signified a change in their status from tenant farmers to landholders. John Gregory worked as a farm laborer in the fields to feed his family. It took everything the Gregorys had—their own and the labor from their eleven children— to buy twelve acres of land which would become their "old home

Van and Mary Woodson home, c. 1930

place." Only one other African American family in their community, the Winns, who owned their own blacksmith shop, had been
able to buy land so soon after the end of slavery. John and Harriet
Gregory lacked the Winns's advantage.[2]

John and Harriet Gregory were met at the courthouse by
Dabney Harris, a white man who had much more in common
with them than he had with most of the members of his own race.
Harris did not hold hundreds of acres of land. He also had not
held slaves before the Civil War. Like the Gregorys, he had purchased a parcel of land from another small holder and, for whatever reason, had decided to do what white men in this section of
Buckingham County did not do: he sold a portion of it to an
African American family.[3]

Knowing how difficult it was for blacks to secure land in this
community, Dabney Harris may have thought that John and Harriet Gregory would do everything in their power to hold onto the
land they had purchased from him. If Harris thought this, he was
wrong. Less than two years after the Harris-Gregory transaction,
both Gregorys were at the Buckingham Courthouse again, this
time selling off some of their hard-worked-for purchase. On this
occasion, however, no whites were parties in the land transaction
and only three dollars sealed the sale. John and Harriet Gregory
conveyed one-half acre of their land to the trustees of the Chief
Cornerstone Baptist Church, allowing a group of African Americans, including themselves, the opportunity to "have church" on
their own land, out of the control, dominion, and sight of the community's whites.[4]

Even though this land transaction was small–only a one-half-
acre plot sold for three dollars–its implication is that African
Americans took a different stance from their white neighbors in
this particular community where land was harder to come by than
money. What this transaction suggests, and the idea this chapter
explores, is that African Americans struggled to buy land and to
hold it. Their goal was not just to own land but to hold land. The
term "landholdership" is used in place of the term "landownership"
because purchased lands became possessions shared with families
and friends. As holders of property, African Americans considered

the land not merely a manifestation of financial security but the cornerstone of their community. As that cornerstone, purchased property became an avenue to personal and group independence. What follows explores these suggestions by examining land transactions and connecting the implications of the transactions to the lives of the buyers of property and to their neighbors and family.

A Different Way of Owning

If the African Americans in this community wanted to hold land for its shared value and not exclusively for its material worth and benefit, were they different from their African Virginian ancestors and contemporaries? Most of what has been written about African Americans' desires and intentions with regard to owning land supports the notion that they, like other Americans, equated land with personal individual freedom. T. H. Breen and Stephen Innes, for example, entitled their study of a seventeenth-century black community *Myne Owne Ground,* from the words written by Anthony Johnson, a black man who after settling a title dispute, asserted, "but now I know myne owne ground and I will worke when I please and play when I please." Breen and Innes conclude that, for colonial African Americans, accumulated property, "even a few cows or pigs, provided legal and social identity in this society; it confirmed individuality." Property, both real estate and personal, was important because it often proved to be the legal tender exchanged to buy the freedom of the slave property holders themselves or the freedom of their loved ones.[5]

Most freedmen shared the goals and aspirations of Anthony Johnson. Whispers that the federal government would grant each slave "forty acres and a mule" brought hope to many African American hearts during Reconstruction. Blacks wanted land to serve the same purpose for them that it had served for white Americans. Many gave pleased nods to Booker T. Washington's assessment that "one of the strongest things that can be said in favor of the colored people is, that in almost every community there are one or two who have shaken off this yoke of slavery and have bought farms of their own and are making money."[6]

In historian James Russell's eyes, Virginia blacks, living in a hostile South, became the eighth wonder of the world, doing what no other people on the face of the earth had done under similar conditions: increase their landholdings tenfold in fifty years.[7] Both Washington and Russell argued that landownership was surely the key to personal and economic freedom. If they recognized that landownership did not ensure freedom and independence, they did not say so publicly.

Why did African Americans equate land with freedom? Why did they consider landownership a panacea in a country where it clearly was not? Historians of the American and African American experience both before and during Reconstruction offer observations which prove useful in explaining why blacks considered land important. Rhys Isaac's assertion that colonial African Americans viewed the land differently from their white counterparts can be used as a key to understanding the African American philosophy concerning landholdership. While the ideal American Anglo home stood separate from its neighbors, often surrounded by land, trees, and formal walkways, African American quarters were usually "small cottages," housing members of work units and then their families. Isaac describes black home sites as a number of huts grouped together and surrounded by land that was cultivated when the enslaved were not in the fields. Whether out of necessity or out of tradition, African Americans kept the West and East African village design, sharing space communally. Those who worked together lived together.[8] One reason landownership became important was that it allowed blacks the opportunity to live together as they had grown accustomed to doing before emancipation.

Herbert Gutman concludes that there was indeed a close connection between post-emancipation land use and familial and kin beliefs. Freedmen wanted to be away from their former work and dwelling places, but did not want to be away from family and friends who either still lived there or close by. It was the realization that kinship members who were either too young or too old to work had to be provided for that made the freedmen consider land as necessary in maintaining and controlling the fate of kin. When blacks realized that white landowners paid and fed only those who worked in their employ, they realized that the workers would have to look out for those who could not work. The possible separation from loved ones became a reality in freedom just as it had been in slavery. Obligations to provide for those to whom the worker was connected, through either blood or care, developed and made landholdership a necessity.[9]

Crandall Shifflett's *Patronage and Poverty* and Jacqueline Jones's *Labor of Love, Labor of Sorrow* both point out that in order to survive freedom, African Americans in the rural South had to adjust their worldview away from majority values of personal gain and individual independence. Writing about a Piedmont Virginia county during the early 1900s, Shifflett concludes that "whole families worked to make a living and perhaps in this way many black families were able to acquire enough to purchase small plots of land" and that "the burden of poverty induced black families to rely on kinship networks to become their brothers' keepers."[10] Jones's observation that "black women and men participated in a rural folk culture based upon group cooperation rather than male competition and the accumulation of goods" supports the idea that if they were to survive, "individualism was a luxury that sharecroppers simply could not afford."[11]

This chapter explores, then, how a group of freed slaves and their descendants set aside havens and homes for themselves. Land transactions and the circumstances that allowed them are examined and discussed illustrating how African Americans, the Gregorys among them, found their own places in an unfriendly land and shared the space.

Only one in five black Belmont farmworker families became landholders. The fortunate ones who did so followed a variety of paths to land acquisition. Several were able to buy an acre or two at first, while others secured tracts of a dozen acres, and still others purchased forty acres and more. None had their way paved for them by the "unique conditions, complex and interwoven" that Loren Schweninger asserts made landownership a real possibility for blacks in Virginia at the turn of the twentieth century. "The long tradition of black proprietorship going back before 1800," he writes, and "the increasing availability of mortgage money; the growth of mutual benefit and insurance societies, and the efforts of black leaders [such as] Congressman John Mercer Langston, editor John Mitchell, and banker Maggie Walker" did not shelter the blacks or pave the way for them in this community.[12] Belmont workers made their own way.

Leaving to Come Back

Isaiah Ayers, or "Zee" as he was called by his family and friends, had to leave his birthplace to earn enough money to own some of it. Unlike the mulattos that Schweninger claims had an advantage over darker-skinned blacks, Ayers received no preferential treatment because he was light enough to pass for white.[13] He married fellow Belmont worker Ella Harris in 1891 and saw her leave her kitchen chores to work with him in James Newman's fields. Newman's handwritten entries under Zee Ayers's name allude to the numerous ways Ayers unsuccessfully tried to become economically secure. He lived at Belmont and worked for his rent there, sharecropped wheat at Sam Ford's place, owned a cow that he bred to increase his stock, and raised and slaughtered hogs for his meat supply. Ayers's rent contract with Newman reflects the keen bargaining the two men engaged in to satisfy their individual expectations:

> 21st Tuesday [Dec. 1890] Zee moved here with my team to feed and attend to teams and stock Sundays as well as other days and to loose anytime or day he does not work—but his findings goes on everyday but he has to attend to teams at all times—even if he does not work in the days.[14]

By agreeing to work for Newman only enough to pay his rent, Ayers was able to determine his own work schedule. This contract allowed Ayers the liberty to use his labor where the wages were highest. Newman no doubt understood this and did not like it. Newman recorded where Ayers spent his time even though he, Newman, was not master of it. One week in August, 1891, for example, Newman wrote that Zee and Ella Ayers went to Baptist Union Church on Monday, Tuesday, Wednesday, and Friday. He did not even speculate where his renter had gone on 15 September; he simply noted that he had gone "off somewhere."[15]

Before her marriage to Zee, Ella Harris had worked in the Belmont house for three years.[16] She had not done any farm work since her first days at Belmont when she and her sister dug potatoes and bound wheat to help pay for a yoke of oxen her father, Davy Harris, had purchased. After her marriage, however, she bound wheat once again and planted corn and worked the melon patches to add to her young family's income.

Marriage and childbirth were costly enterprises that both Ella and Zee worked to afford. They lost twenty-seven of the thirty-eight cents Ella had earned when Newman charged them that much to rent one of Belmont's horses. Zee needed transportation on 1 December 1891 to fetch the doctor who delivered their first child. The wagon pulled by Newman's mare Mayflower was used to pick up Mrs. Jennie Tyree, a black woman who would stay with Ella after the baby's birth, and its use cost them thirty-eight cents, more than Ella had earned planting corn.[17] They must have known that a different strategy was necessary if they were to get a place of their own.

Ayers family history contends that Zee, Ella, and the newborn Walker left the Belmont neighborhood and moved to West Virginia where Zee found work at higher wages in the coal mines. He made enough money to support Ella and the three babies born there, and to save for Buckingham County land.[18] By 1896, Zee was back within sight of Belmont, his family, and friends. Olive Ayers, a white man (unrelated, as far as is now known) in the community, agreed to sell him forty acres of land, for one dollar an acre.[19] Zee Ayers had his forty acres and would go on to get his mule.

Six years after his first purchase, Ayers added five and one-half more acres to his holdings.[20] Three years after that he witnessed his wife and sister-in-law, Amanda Brown, sign a deed bringing twenty-five additional acres into his family.[21] At five-year intervals the women became the holders of two additional tracts, one of sixty acres and another of twenty-five.[22] Around this time, Ella and Amanda also started to give away small portions of the land they had acquired to one of Zee's younger brothers, George. In 1917, the two women gave George Ayers sixteen acres, and then two years later, twenty-five more acres. In 1921, Zee Ayers extended the family's holdings for the last time by bringing seventeen and one-half more acres under his family's name.[23]

One of Zee and Ella's granddaughters has much to say about their landholdings and what they did with them. Julia Ayers Anderson says that her grandfather owned over eight hundred acres and was able to "get ahold of that much land" because he was in fact a white man and hence did not experience the same difficulties his black neighbors and relatives did in acquiring acreage. According to Anderson, Zee was not a "hoarder" and shared what he had with others, giving some of the land away and letting others live on other parts of it for little or no charge. She is able to name different families in the community who lived on Zee and Ella Ayers's land and in the dwellings they had built on the land.

Some of what Anderson has heard about her grandparents is remarkably accurate while some is not.

Zee Ayers's light skin did not make him a white man to the whites in the community. He is listed in the census as a mulatto. All of his land deeds and tax records are listed in the "colored" portion of the land deed books in the back, following the listings of the white population's holdings. He was in fact a very light-skinned African American who may have been fathered by one of two white men with the same surname in his community. The family has no record of who Zee Ayers's parents were. They are not listed in the family Bible in the early entries written out in Ella Ayers's hand. Zee himself could not read or write. Zee was in fact lighter than his brother George, who is listed as black in the census. There are no birth certificates for either of the men on file at the Buckingham County Courthouse.[24]

Zee and Ella Ayers owned 173 acres, not 800. Because their family had one of the largest landholdings among blacks in the community, their holdings may have seemed larger than they really were. Besides holding so much land, the two did in fact do remarkable things with it. They claimed the Homestead Exemption Act when securing other property or mortgaging their tobacco crops, something other blacks without the advantage of landholdings were unable to do. (Because the Ayerses had enough property to be considered economically viable, they did not have to put liens on their lands in order to get loans. They were considered better credit risks.) They took other blacks with them to the courthouse and had them witness the signing of the land deeds and transfers they signed, going against area tradition of having whites in the community or at the courthouse bear witness to the transfer of property.[25] They also rented dwellings to other blacks that were remarkably better than those found on the property of whites, where most black renters had to settle for simply a place to stay. One of these single-story wood houses is still standing with its rock and stone fireplace intact. A center hallway separates the front room and kitchen from two sleeping rooms at the back. Like many of the houses built during the early twentieth century, it sits back off the road and is within walking distance of a spring where water could be "toted" to the dwelling.[26]

The Gregory Family Way

The John Gregorys did not have to go to West Virginia to earn the $30 to buy the nucleus of the family homestead. John and Harriet used their own and their eleven children's labor. This strategy kept the family together, but it also took an extended period of time to bear fruit. It took the family nine years of work as freedmen to buy twelve acres of land. The family would work for almost twenty-five more years to purchase another parcel, this time a tract fifty acres larger than their first.[27] The deed book lists the names of the oldest family male, John, and one of the youngest, Taylor, as the property owners. This well represents the way that the entire family participated in holding this family land, from the oldest person in the family to the youngest.

By 1900 the Gregorys knew all too well that in order to progress and stay safe, they would have to hold the land they worked. Incidents James Newman recorded in his farm account ledgers support this explicitly. Newman had known John and Harriet Gregory and their sons and daughters since at least 1870 when the area census taker listed their names under his in the federal record. The Gregory sons–William, Henry, Sam, and Alexander–had worked for him. The Gregory daughters, Judy and Kate, had done the same. Newman knew them to be good workers but he still had his complaints, some of which he made known to them. In 1889, for example, James Newman must have said something to William Gregory's son Taylor, who had followed his father's example and gone to Belmont to work for Newman. Newman hired Taylor to do farm work, such as burning plant patches and putting in seed for $6.50 a month. Twenty-six-year-old Taylor must have felt that either the money was too little, or that Newman's work too hard, because he left after only five days. At first Newman wrote that Taylor had "quit and went to McKenna's because he sent for him." (James McKenna was a local farmer who owned a two-hundred-acre farm several miles from Belmont.) In the notation to himself, Newman rationalized that Taylor's leaving, even during the peak work time of spring planting, was all right because Taylor was "too slow for his price."[28] Newman did not admit, even to himself, that Taylor left his employ because he wanted to do so. Newman kept in his mind that Taylor had left because of a white man's actions, not the black man's resolve owing to his own dissatisfaction.

Taylor did return several times to work for Newman over the next ten years. Most of the time, however, he came back with his father, William, and did "evening work" at Belmont after they had completed their work days elsewhere. Their pay was in both cash and foodstuffs, such as butter and Winesap apples, luxuries for their tables. In 1894, William came back to Belmont without his son and helped another black man, Peter Winfrey, dig Pattie Newman's grave. Newman paid William Gregory thirty-five pounds of oatmeal for the half day it took to shovel out the hole in Belmont soil. The oatmeal would provide for the Gregory family table, but would not directly add to the funds needed to secure land.[29]

In May and June 1895, the Gregory family had their last run-in with Newman and never returned to work at Belmont after that. William's younger brother, Sam, had a special relationship with James Newman's cook at that time, Sarah Woodson. Sam purchased a ham for Sarah, paying $1.76 for the fifteen and one-half pounds of meat. He worked off the cost of his gift by first "dropping corn" and then "putting in hen manure" over the kernels as the second step in the planting process. Sarah, in turn, purchased one quart of grape wine for him, costing twenty-five cents, one-tenth of her month's earnings, and then a new pair of cashimere pants. But in late June, Sarah had an argument with James Newman's nephew, Stephen Trent, which was when the trouble started. Trent slapped Sarah Woodson and Sam

Gregory stood up for her. Gregory fought and beat Trent. Angry, and perhaps afraid of being turned over to the authorities, Sam Gregory went to James Newman, and asked Newman to speak to Trent about the incident. Newman recorded his account of the incident this way:

> June 24 Monday, Sam Gregory followed Stephen W. Trent and took up for Sarah Woodson because Stephen slapped her and gave him [Stephen Trent] a good beating.
> June 28 To my services for him in full after his fight to see Stephen (his request)   25
> To cash pd. him in full, all demands to date forever   87.
> I am done hiring him now and forever.

Sarah Woodson also left Newman's employ, never to return.[30]

Three years after this incident, in 1898, the Gregorys were able to once again pool their resources, buying enough land for them to all live on and farm.[31] Four generations would eventually live on this family land, all in the same area as the original twelve-acre purchase. The land bordered and surrounded the Chief Cornerstone and Cedar Baptist churches. Deeds were listed under the names of family males of each generation. John and Harriet's sons, William, Henry, and Alexander would hold 96.3 acres between them. John and Harriet would gain 50 additional acres in their names.[32] William's son Taylor secured 35 acres under his own name while also being listed as jointly holding land with his grandfather. Alexander's son James had fifty acres listed in his name. The 1920 census lists William's grandson John III residing on Gregory land with his wife and their children, making the Gregory homestead a place for four generations to live and work.[33]

Ben and Nannie Woodson's Family

If Nannie and Ben Woodson had been able to use the labor of their eighteen children, they could have become landholders like the Gregorys. They were not able to do so. Six of their children died before reaching adulthood. Others married and moved away from home, starting their own families, and Ben died, leaving Nannie with children at home to raise alone.[34]

Like the Gregorys, Ben Woodson lived close to the Belmont Plantation after emancipation. Unlike John Gregory, Woodson did not head his own household; at twenty-one years of age, he still lived with his parents, Charles and Rachel, and five siblings. None of them could read or write. By 1880, however, Ben Woodson headed his own household and was married to the former Nannie Peaks. The couple was listed in 1880 as having six children aged fourteen years to one year old. Even though Woodson had remained in his parents' home, he and Nannie were parents to two sons born before they were listed in the census as living together.[35] Their oldest sons, Robert and William, joined father Ben in the Belmont fields.

Ben Woodson appears to have worked as hard as John and Harriet Gregory's sons at Belmont. Woodson never lived on Newman's place, but would take a day's work there when he could. For three days in August 1890, for example, he cleaned and grubbed melon patches. The next week, he cut the early millet crop when it was sunny or weeded Pattie Newman's garden when it was not. After cutting millet he shucked corn for two days. Three months later Woodson "sowed wheat from "8 1/2 till night." The following July he could be found, "laying by corn" to earn forty cents and some flour.[36]

To earn additional cash and foodstuffs, Ben started bringing his sons with him to work. When he sent them alone, Newman often wrote that Robert or William had "1 hour lost every morning" by arriving an hour after the arrival time Newman set. But Woodson needed his sons to help him purchase work animals to plow land he sharecropped elsewhere. Four days after Christmas 1891, Woodson purchased a yoke of oxen from James Newman for forty dollars. Three months later, Woodson realized that the oxen were more than he could afford and traded them back to Newman in exchange for a pair of steers. Newman charged fifteen dollars less for the steers than he had for the oxen. By sowing oats and working around the farm, the three Woodsons paid off the balance the family owed.[37]

Newman still had serious complaints about the ways in which the Woodson sons worked. On the first day of September 1893, Newman recorded that Ben's "son William [was only] pretending to plow in oats–but he came 1 hour by sun and quit for no cause in eve and left ox team in field." None of the Woodsons worked at Belmont during the following three months, and when they returned Ben did the work "getting 602 pine rails at 40 cents per 100."[38]

The Woodsons worked hard and did not waste. The hen that Newman listed as "killed by wezel this morning" was sold to Ben Woodson for twenty-five cents and eaten by his family.[39] If providing for such a large family had been hard during Ben Woodson's lifetime, it became more difficult when Nannie became a widow in 1900. The first census of this century shows Nannie Woodson as heading a family with seven children, aged nineteen to six, and living on rented property. She no longer lived next to her husband's father and brother but had moved to another place still within the community. By 1910 her son Van would have started his own family, and two nephews and one niece would join her household and live with her four children still at home. She continued living on a rented farm. An event that happened in her son Benjamin's life most probably edged her on to get a place for her family to live.[40]

Sometime between 1900 and 1910, Benny had a run-in with area whites.[41] The family was living on the Caryswood plantation, when John Trent, James Newman's nephew and Stephen Trent's brother, "got after Benny about something." Family legend has it that "the something" had to do with a white woman. John Trent chased Benny into the cabin that he lived in with his mother and siblings. Benny, afraid for his life, climbed quickly up the ladder to the sleeping loft and jumped out the second-story window, onto the ground intending to escape with his life. The hard landing onto the ground twisted and broke a bone in his right leg. He could not run to get away, but John Trent surmised that the leg would be reminder enough for him to mend his ways. Bones would often "work their way out of his skin" and he would save them all in a match box, fearing that he could not get into heaven without all of the bones in his body. His mother, Nannie, part Native American, is said to have introduced and shared this belief with her son.

Benny left Caryswood for a time and lived nearby on another white man's place, joining his brother Van, sister-in-law Mary Wade, and their children at Union Hill. By 1911 he was back home with Nannie and the next year moved onto their first home place of two acres. His mother by that time was fifty-seven years old. She paid seventeen dollars an acre for the small piece of property.[42] Was she so determined to have her own place for her family that she paid ten times more than the going rate for land, or was it that the only land she could buy was outside of the community in which she lived and the whites who sold her the property charged her a higher cost, hearing about what had happened to her son? It could have been either or both of these reasons.

Woodson would buy another parcel of land before her death in 1917.[43] It was larger than her first purchase, but still small, only fourteen acres. She listed all of her children still living at home as joint owners, holders with her of the land. Three years after she died, her children bought another tract of land, fifteen acres, and listed her name along with theirs on the deed.[44] Family members continue to live on that land today.

Lewis Morris

In 1905, one of Nannie Woodson's neighbors, Lewis Morris, a single man without children, decided to become a landholder. He headed a household comprised of his sisters and their children. Morris would have been familiar with what occurred at the Caryswood plantation because he had lived there off and on for all of his life and knew the Woodson family very well. Two of his sisters' children had married Benny Woodson's brothers. And like the Gregory and Woodson boys, he had supplemented his father's work on James Newman's place. The contract that Newman negotiated with Lewis's father even mentions the then teenager by name,

> 1896
>
> Dec. 16th. Alexander Morris come and bargained to live with me for the year 1897 on the following conditions. He to work my team–oxen–and land on shares–half and half. Newman to furnish the team and land and feed for the team and Alex Morris and son Lewis to do the labor and find themselves when working on their share crop–

and Newman agrees to pay Morris $25 for 3 days in each week which is half of his time during the year and to find his one man's rations during the year which would be 1 1/2 gallons meals and 1 1/2 lbs bacon each week and he, Morris to attend to feed all my team that I keep on my farm–horses, cows, oxen etc.. and I find him my double quarter 4 room house and garden during the time is working on shares and while hired to me during the year and he to get his wood he uses in his house in his own time but has the use of my team. And Newman has to get or have gotten his [own] fire wood used in his house.[45]

Lewis helped his father pile four wagon loads of family furniture and drive it to Belmont, 17 December 1896. From the beginning of their time at Belmont, Lewis Morris must have known that with the amount of supplies and food his family purchased from Newman's storehouse, they would never save enough funds to have a place of their own. At the end of the Morris's first six months at Belmont, the father and son had earned $17.68 and had incurred $14.16 worth of debts. They were charged for the hire of Newman's mare Nelly, bushels of corn, buttons, bone and potash fertilizer, and one black secondhand man's coat. The $3.52 that Newman passed over to Lewis's father soon found its way back into Newman's pocket when the family needed corn, and the use of the oxen to take the corn to the mill, two horses to take them to church and two "large young chickens."[46]

Lewis Morris may have been frustrated by not being able to save any of the Belmont money they earned, but this frustration probably took a second place in his mind compared to the uneasiness that came between Newman and his father over the quarter they rented on Belmont land. Newman offered his side of the disagreement by writing

Oct. 9th [1898] Alex Morris refused to move from quarter at yard to house on hill as the bargain was he to move up there and work on shares–bargain made 17th March 1898 but he kept agreeing to move week after week but did not and today he got 3 teams and moved his family and things to E.P. Page's. He told me this morning he was going off to get a place to put his daughter's fine things–I went S[unday] School and when I got back in evening he and all *were* gone not letting me know a thing about it.–Jas. Newman[47]

E. P. Page's place was, of course, the Caryswood plantation where Benny Woodson would jump out of the window trying to escape Page's son-in-law, John Trent. One of Lewis's nieces concluded that the white people in their community around the turn of the century were "real mean back then."[48] Lewis Morris went from the frying pan into the fire and stayed there for twenty-three years until he could get his hands on some land.

When the 1900 census was taken, Alexander and Charlotte Morris lived at Caryswood with a daughter Annie, their son Lewis, a son George, and three grandchildren. Only six of their twelve children still lived. By 1910 both of them would be dead and Lewis would take over as head of the household which still included his sister Annie, but which now also included her three children, Charlotte, aged nine, Martha, aged four, and Royal, aged two.[49] Lewis supported the family by working the same plantation land his father, mother, and maternal grandfather had worked before emancipation. "Sis" Annie would also work in the Caryswood kitchen, a place she, too, was no stranger to. Her children, like the slave children before them, played in the yards next to the ice house and behind the smokehouse.

It took Lewis Morris about twenty years, but he saved sixty dollars, enough to "put his hands on a piece of Caryswood land" before he died. The real estate that Lewis purchased included a dwelling, valued at $28.[50] The house was not very big, but it was big enough for the Morris family to sleep in at night and it suited them just fine.

An incident about three years before Lewis Morris's death illustrates how he felt about "white people's things."[51] On the last day of October 1939, one of his nieces had been preparing for a big day, her youngest daughter's wedding, for weeks. The table was set for people to come inside and eat after the ceremony. Lewis came in and started "cutting up" as usual. He observed, "You all think that you've set a nice table. Looks like a white folks table to me. Yes this looks just like a white folks table to me."

Without saying another word, Lewis, who everyone by this time suspected had had a "taste too much," turned over a big bowl of peas onto the tablecloth and proceeded to eat them directly from "the table just like a pig." The women standing around were too angry to speak. When Lewis finished "his meal," he wiped his mouth on the tablecloth and left. The women removed and replaced the tablecloth, refilled the bowl of peas, and reset the table, all the while saying, "You can't do nothin' with Uncle Lewis."

George Holman

Most Belmont workers were never able to engage in such antics on land not under their own control. Most were like George Holman who signed on to work at Belmont in 1889 and was never able to own or control a place that did not belong to white people. Like twenty-seven other Belmont heads of households, he was never able to secure land. As a fifteen-year-old in 1870, he lived on the rented property of white farmer Edward Shepherd and worked as a farm laborer.[52]

The 1900 census lists George Holman, his wife Manda, and their seven children, living on the same property Holman had worked thirty years before. Edward Shepherd, Holman's employer, now owned the land he had rented thirty years before. George Holman was there once again as one of the hands. In thirty years, Holman had not gained an advantage. He had obtained only a large family and all of the responsibilities that came with growing children.[53]

Robert Bryant

One of James Newman's white laborers was also unable to buy land. Robert Bryant, who also had a number of unpleasant experiences with Newman, married two women whose families owned land and gained an advantage Holman and others who could not or did not marry into landholding families never had.

Unlike the Woodsons and Morrises, who had to retreat onto the property of another white man, Bryant could continue to live on his in-laws' property, and even have his mother and sister live there too. When Nannie Bryant, his first wife, died, however, he was faced with a problem of not having a place to live. Bryant married another woman, Bell Creasy, twenty-five years his junior, whose family also owned land. In the 1910 census, Bryant is listed as living on the Creasy homestead headed by his wife's twenty-three-year-old nephew.

Bryant had fathered three children by her during the twenty years they had been married. Even though the sixty-year-old Bryant had added to the Creasy clan, they did not consider him head of it but allowed him to stay on the place with his second wife and their children.[54]

The Winn Family

The only African American family in the Belmont community that in any way resembles the landowners Loren Schweninger discusses in *Black Property Owners* are the Winns. Henry Winn's name is recorded in the first extant land book for Buckingham County. Like Virginia blacks who lived closer to cities and larger towns, both Henry Winn and his wife could read. Henry Winn's relationship with James Newman was very unusual. Newman appeared to need Winn's services as much as Winn needed his. Newman traded and bartered with Winn for the blacksmith's services. On 4 May 1887, Newman passed on "400 lbs sheaf oats" to Winn as payment for "welding 2 new axles and repairing springs etc. of my old buggy."[55] Winn was the only man of either race who accepted a subscription to a newspaper for payment of a debt from Newman. On 17 June 1884, Newman wrote on Winn's account sheet:

> . . . Cash pd your sub. to Weekly Slate for 6 months in
> club of 10   39¢

Winn was also the only black man Newman ever provided with a written receipt. Newman confirmed,

> Nov. 1st [1887] I gave my written obligation to Henry Winn to pay him soon for Willie or Jim Langhorn $7 on the ox bought by Jim Langhorn of Winn.[56]

The four Winn children continued to live on the twenty-four-acre original homestead after 1915 when Dolly purchased seventy-three additional acres. The 1920 census lists four Winn households grouped together next to each other. By this time, both Henry and Dolly Winn had died. Their son John, who also could read and write, had taken over his father's blacksmithing business. John and his wife Lillian, a mulatto, had three mulatto children, Russell, Westa, and Harrold. John's brother Marcellus and his wife, Josie (also a mulatto), shared the family home which Dolly had purchased in 1915 when she was a widow and sixty years old. The house had an assessed tax value of $219. John farmed the place. Brother James would live on the next farm over with his wife and their two sons and have his occupation listed as a farmer also. Farmers or not, the Winns were exceptional. Even though they never achieved the quality of life of the upper-class whites in their community, they would live better than most blacks in the area because they had needed skills, a smaller family, and had owned land longer than other African Americans living in their community.[57]

While most African Americans who had worked on the Belmont Farm were unable to "get their hands on a little piece of land," a courageous, hard-working, and fortunate few were successful. Unlike blacks in other Virginia communities closer to cities and larger towns, these rural Piedmont blacks purchased only enough land to allow them a shelter from the storms of the difficult times of the late 1800s and early twentieth century. African American single men, widowed women, parents of young families who had been brave enough to leave the area to amass funds, and older couples with working sons and daughters were all able to secure homesteads but they took different paths towards "home."

Out of the thirty-five black and white families that provided Belmont with workers, only seven of them were able to purchase land between twenty and fifty years after emancipation. This does not mean that others did not try. Charles Swann, who worked for James Newman off and on for more than ten years, staked his entire share-cropped tobacco harvest after World War I to obtain funds he planned to use to buy land. His luck and tobacco failed and he ended up in court losing everything.[58] He had waived homestead exemption rights.[59]

Those who were able to secure land did not use it to add to their own personal wealth. Unlike their fellow Virginian, Anthony Johnson, who had lived two hundred years before, and their contemporaries presented in the Schweninger study, the African Americans in this community appeared satisfied with land that was titled in their names and over which they could exercise decisive control.

With land so hard to come by, blacks in this community did what Zee and Ella Ayers did and what the Gregorys before them had done. They shared what they had with family and friends and when they owned land they held onto it as a place of refuge (even if only in garrets and legal loopholes), away from men like John and Stephen Trent and James Newman. They watched white men like Robert Bryant who was able to stay on a friendly place even if he did not own or hold the land. They wanted to have the same advantage. And they did.

4. Getting Things

❧ Olivia Jane Tyree Swann was one of the first, if not the first person, in her family to acquire reading as a skill. A photograph taken in about 1920 captures her as a young married woman with a growing family. While most of her time was probably absorbed taking care of them, on this occasion she took time out to dress for the camera, as did her husband, John Swann. They had "gotten things." The camera found them in their finery.

Olivia Jane Tyree Swann, c. 1920

A dying woman who had been hungry all of her life asked for a few crackers so that she would not have to die–the way she had lived–with an empty stomach. A man, angered by the sight of a relative's table set with fancy "white folks" dishes, dumped the contents of one dish onto the fancy tablecloth and ate the food directly from the cloth. A farmhand loaded all of his family's furniture into a wagon and drove off one "white man's place" to another's. As he left the plantation, he called back over his shoulder that he was leaving to find a more fitting place for "his daughter's fine things." An unmarried freed woman pledged to harvest a meadow of wheat to earn the funds necessary to buy a cure for the spasms that shook her body and unsettled her life.[1]

Each of these instances is an example of this community's black rural consumerism that came to be a part of the New South. They represent the importance various kinds of consumer objects held in the lives of African Americans. Food, or the lack of it, European-influenced tableware and linens, furniture and clothes, and

John Swann, c. 1920

even medical care, all held places of importance in the hearts and minds of blacks who were decades or less away from slavery.

This chapter explores the buying habits of individuals who were once bought themselves under a system of chattel slavery. It discusses consumption in the rural South in the decades following the Civil War, the ways that people "got things," and how this process influenced and shaped this community's culture. What follows attempts to identify and describe the existence of community buying patterns over time, and examines whether buying patterns in this community followed recognized trends for blacks in other parts of the South.

What Was

Shortly after the Civil War ended, a freedman encountered the man who had held him in bondage. The black man, careful not to challenge a white man by looking him in the eye, averted his glance to a two-railed fence next to which the white man stood, and muttered, "top rail on the bottom now." The Civil War and black emancipation meant the loss of thousands of dollars of personal wealth for white slaveholders, but did they knock the top rail off the fence, upsetting economies in recognizable ways?

In 1870, the Pages of Union Hill and Caryswood, like the Trents and Gannaways of Belmont, were worth only a fraction of what they had been ten years and a war earlier. Edward Page boasted of personal property amounting to $30,000 in 1860. In that same year, his father's estate, which listed forty-seven slaves, had a value exceeding $65,000. While James Newsman's father-in-law Theodorick Gannaway was not as well off as the Pages, his eighteen slaves comprised the bulk of his $18,000 in personal property worth and allowed for a comfortable life for him and his family.[2] In 1870, Edward Page told the census taker that his personal wealth only amounted to $1,000. His mother, who still headed his father's estate, listed her personal property as $3,000, over $60,000 less than it had been ten years before. T. C. Gannaway's widow had only $500 in personal property listed next to her name.[3]

These plantation owners had lost human beings worth thousands of dollars. Gone were Albert and Sidney Harris and their son Thomas, who, together, had been assessed as contributing $1,500 to the worth of Edward Page's father's estate in 1854. Gone, too, were Moses and Mary Wade and their children Jane, Jerry, and Van, who had contributed $2,500 more. Three generations of women–Jenny, her daughter Maria, and an unnamed granddaughter (Nannie, who would grow up and marry Ben Woodson), appraised as worth $1,300–were freed persons too, no longer claimed as adding value to someone else's purchasing power. Such changes significantly altered the buying patterns of this community.[4]

The Civil War and emancipation were not the only absorbers of personal wealth and buying power. Death had claimed John C. Page, and his lifetime of making good financial decisions, in 1853.[5] Poor management had done its part in adjusting the Gannaway family's abilities to consume. When Theodorick Gannaway unwisely invested thousands of dollars of his brother's estate, over which he was trustee, and lost it and his nephew's security in the process, he permanently weakened his charge's financial security and buying power. He did this before a shot was ever fired or a single person freed.[6] Almost eighty years after Gannaway's death, one of his descendants recalled that Gannaway had "reduced the condition of the farm greatly, caused the slaves to be poorly clad and fed, and brought about their ill health and the consequent hiring out of many of them to indifferent masters at low wages."[7]

No matter what the reason, Pattie Newman's cousin Richard W. Gannaway, her father's charge who had lost not only his father but his inheritance as well between 1860 and 1870, spoke for many when he lamented, "sickness in the house, the wear and tear of trying to save something out of this terrible war which will be fought on the plantations for many years, trouble with the slaves who expect manna from the North while they sleep in their cabins" plagued the South.[8] To say that this community after the Civil War did not afford the comforts slavery had provided would be an understatement.

What Came to Be

Even with such consequences, the realities of freedom challenged the notion that the bottom rail could ever be on the top. According to Roger L. Ransom and Richard Sutch, slavery constructed the New South's economics of African American consumerism in unique ways even though the actual purchasing power of blacks increased only 11.5 percent after emancipation. On an average, blacks could spend only $5 a year per family member on clothing, tobacco, and other cash items.[9] In this community, economic realities and necessities made for unmet wants and unobtainable wishes in many instances. Adult male workers on Page's farm earned $85 a year. A husband and wife team together earned between $115 and $145 yearly. A man with two sons who labored with him in the fields drew top dollar of $185 a year. Page rented Caryswood slave cabins to freedmen for $30 a year, bringing a significant portion of what he paid out in labor back into his own pockets. People had to have a place to live. Everything had a cost. Page and Newman advanced grooms-to-be $2 for marriage licenses and dollars to pay for the ceremony. Midwives charged $2 to attend the births of children born to these unions.[10]

Wants and needs became the same thing. Because many slaveholders had limited the amount of food they provided the people they enslaved, many African Americans suffered hunger all of their lives.[11] Many led lives similar to Polly Wade's, who, once free, tried without success to keep hunger at bay.

Edward T. Page's recorded the purchases of twenty-three individuals, married couples, and families he employed in 1867 and 1868, illustrating the importance freed people placed on food and clothing.[12] His accounts tell Ransom and Sutch's tale, but with a different twist. Ransom and Sutch found that freedmen consumed more meats in their diets than they had before emancipation, with meat making up a greater portion of their diets than vegetables or cereals.[13] Out of the twenty-three individuals and family groups Page employed, nineteen of them purchased food from him with the money they earned. It does not appear, however, that earning $85 to $185 a year allowed them the privilege of buying large quantities of meat. When Wilson Morris purchased a pig from another black man, Davy Harris, in 1883, the $2.73 cost of it equaled more than one-half his monthly Belmont wage of $6.80 a month.[14] Page sold more corn and wheat to his workers than he did bacon.[15] The 1870 agricultural census eliminates the possibility that these families raised their own livestock and did not have to use their earnings to buy meat from Page, Newman, or anyone else. The folks who worked for Page did not claim that they owned pigs, cows, or sheep. (In 1867–1868 only one freedman, Nelson Peaks, used his wages to buy a horse and a cow. By 1870 his livestock were either dead or in someone else's hands. The Agricultural and Production Schedule does not list Peaks as having any livestock.) It appears that chicken, fish, and wild game supplied the meat for their tables.[16]

James Newman, a new patron in 1869, listed only one worker purchase in this early 1867–1869 period. William Gregory bought three yards of domestic cloth from Newman. This transaction supports the notion that purchases made soon after the Civil War were primarily for food and clothing.[17]

Ransom and Sutch's suggestion, that as blacks increased the amount of meat they consumed, they also regularly added candy, whiskey, and cheese to their intake, also does not hold completely true for the blacks in this community.[18] In 1867 and 1868, while seven of the twenty-three Caryswood workers purchased whiskey, and four of them purchased molasses, they do not appear to have been able to afford processed sugar or other sweets. Sugar was the least purchased food item. Black workers purchased salt more frequently than they purchased sugar. There are no recorded purchases for candy or cheese of any kind during the first years of freedom for the men, women, and children who worked at Caryswood.[19]

In This Place

This community's black population did not follow Ransom and Sutch's proposed trends with regard to the choice and purchasing of clothing, either. According to Ransom and Sutch, when newly freed persons had the opportunity to clothe themselves as they chose, "brightly colored calicoes, cottonades, denims, shoes, hats, brass jewelry and head handkerchiefs" quickly replaced their formerly plain fare.[20] Page's account records in his Leather Pocket Notebook suggest that a change in color and quality of freed people's attire took years, and not weeks or months, to appear. Necessity and practicality seemed to rule the day in 1867 and 1868. During that time, all but three of Page's newly freed persons and families purchased cloth, but they selected blue, black, and white fabrics, matching these shades with larger purchases of osnaburg (a rough cloth blend of wool and cotton, often called slave cloth because it was used so frequently to make garments worn by enslaved people). They appeared, however, to be more intent on covering their heads and feet than their backs; the most frequently purchased ready-made clothing items were socks and hats. Seventeen out of the twenty-three purchased boots, shoes, or the soles for shoes. Several families purchased more than one pair. One man obtained a pair of shoes for his father but not for himself.

Emancipation also refigured the times when blacks acquired material objects. Gone were the days when Christmas and a new year meant a new pair of shoes and several ready-made osnaburg garments and when folks "lived for" Christmas time.[21] The first Christmases of freedom did not provide material gain but became a time of settling up, with many walking away with a small amount of cash after their farm and store accounts had been paid. Male and female Belmont workers in 1886, for example, often ended up with less than a dollar in cash at the end of their contracts, which ended in late December, either a few days before or after Christmas. Judy Gregory walked away with twenty-two cents, her sister Kate with sixty cents, Peter Winfrey with twenty-seven cents, and Wilson Morris with only a nickel. Those who faired better—such as Nelson White who received $7.12 and Julia Ann White who probably placed her $3.65 in an apron pocket—proved to be the exception and not the rule. A year later, White's replacement, America Powell, left Belmont with only thirty-seven cents.[22]

Acquisitions were spread out over longer periods and were connected to the worker's immediate needs, not a set holiday season. In spreading purchases out over longer periods and using credit, blacks followed established community patterns of consumption. Charles Orser explains that after tenant farming or sharecropping for a whole year, blacks were seldom eager to settle up with merchants and landowners. The money they earned was not long in their pockets. Even though "cash after settling" was often very low, freedmen were encouraged to spend their cash on unnecessary items. Tactics such as this increased black dependence on white suppliers of goods because blacks were quickly rendered cash-poor.[23] For Caryswood and Belmont workers, their cash-poor status was the result of buying food and goods they needed during the year. Their lack of cash just seemed to propel them more quickly into new contracts with the hope that they would end up in a better financial situation at another year's end.

Ransom and Sutch recognize that freedmen consumed luxuries all year and not just at settling time, and that they "exchanged a fraction of their potential income for 'free time': time for leisure, housekeeping, child care—in short, time for all the activities of men and women other than those designed to earn material income."[24] It was through the consumption of leisure that blacks demonstrated desires to duplicate the patterns of other Americans. After emancipation, blacks were able to purchase what many whites took for granted—the ability to watch while others worked. Male and female heads of households decided who would work where and for how long. Not working at all was not an option these freed people seemed to consider.

Blacks in this New South community shared "a love of things" with those on the other side of the color line. James Newman was a paragon of consumerism who did not attempt to conceal the fact. He appeared to lure workers to buy objects as well. His years as storekeeper and pharmacist made him keenly aware of the wants of others. He became a man who knew how to get things. Shopping trips to Richmond and Farmville and mail-order catalogs supplied him with a wealth of items he could trade for a day's labor or sell outright. Caryswood owners wanted what could be bought, too. Numerous shop receipts are a testament to Elizabeth Coupland Page's shopping trips to a dry goods store in Farmville and her frequently satisfied yearnings for things for herself and home. On one occasion, characteristic of many others, she purchased eight yards of linen, one yard of calico, and wallpaper, paying for her wants with cash. Most of Pattie Newman's purchases were for herself—not for her home. On one occasion she bought a pair of shoes that cost the same as one of her workers had paid for a pig. Her $2 bonnet and $1.31 parasol indicate that she considered it important to protect herself from the tanning power of the sun. No black women purchased parasols.[25]

Family age and composition appears to have been the main determinants of what Caryswood's freed people purchased. Nathan Woodson, who was twenty-three years old in 1868, had a wife and three children under the age of five. His $85 annual wage paid his $30 rent to Page and purchased his family one pair of shoes, socks, seven yards of osnaburg, molasses, corn—and an unspecified quantity of whiskey for him. It also allowed him to pay a $24 general store bill. The Henry Harris family had almost twice the buying power of Woodson's young family with only one out-of-the-home worker. Harris and his three sons earned $183 annually laboring for Page. This income supported their family of seven and purchased almost fifty yards of cloth for them, twenty-three pounds of bacon, bushels of corn, and a ready-made dress for the mother of the family. It also paid a modest West Brothers general store account of $5.46. Henry Harris's parents both worked for Page in 1868 even though they were in their late sixties and early seventies. Their $145 combined income bought them three bushels of wheat, paid their $25 account at Hall's General Store twelve miles away, and paid for whiskey the day after Christmas.[26]

Because the bottom rail was never permanently at the top, the freedman's desire to consume was frustrating, leading many outside of the law. According to Edward Ayers, consumer goods represented what southerners demanded but could not purchase. Consumption was a reminder of what they wanted to be but were not.[27] People often found ways outside the law to satisfy the yearnings they could not legally fulfill. Newman's journal and account books are sprinkled with notations indicating that he believed that his workers were stealing his property, breaking his padlocks, and walking off with items that did not belong to them.

Residents of this community would have known of two local country stores, the West General Store, next door to Belmont at Gravel Hill, and the Hall General Store, about twelve miles away on the north-to-south stagecoach line. The Wests were not newcomers to Buckingham County. An established farmer by 1810, John S. West with eight children younger than ten and eleven enslaved blacks, raised wheat, corn, and tobacco. Over the next forty years, one of West's sons and his grandsons met the needs of the community by offering blacksmithing and cartering services and hiring out vehicles to those in need of transportation. Between 1850 and 1860, John West II increased his personal wealth from $1,000 to $4,000. His general store became successful enough to permit him to stop farming altogether by 1860. West's slave holdings increased only slightly in this same period. In 1850 he held what appears to have been a small enslaved family with a thirty-year-old man, a younger woman, and a twelve-year-old child. The six blacks he held in 1860 accounted for a small portion of his $4,000 in personal property worth.[28]

The Halls, likewise, were not large-scale farmers. The two Hall brothers joined together and opened a general store, blacksmith shop, and carriage/wagon-making establishment in the 1850s. Both stores were worth approximately the same amount of money and did business with the same number of people. Before emancipation, they even employed one of the community's free blacks, John Winn.[29]

For Page and Newman workers, these country stores became a concrete reminder of want and an indicator of social and economic progress. The availability of the one local general store and another a wagon ride away allowed blacks the opportunity not to have to directly go to their employers for all of their purchases all of the time. This ability to obtain needed and wanted goods from someone other than the landowners and employers permitted blacks to take one step away from slavery and economic dependence to their employers. But it was not a big step. Page and Newman both paid store account balances, deducting the funds from workers' wages. Only one of Page's workers did not use a portion of his earnings to satisfy a store account. Newman recorded in his diaries that black and white farmhands went with him to both local stores and one in Farmville. There is no indication that blacks ever accompanied him to Richmond or places more distant, such as Washington, D.C., or Baltimore. Newman maintained a distance so as not to give someone his advantage.

The general store seemed to draw Newman more often at certain times of the year. April, May, and June found him there frequently, often one day after another. On these occasions he seldom went alone. Young and old blacks went with him. Others sent him with what he termed "verbal orders" of their requests.

Even through economic depressions in 1873 and 1893, consumerism rose steadily during the last decades of the nineteenth century. Country people purchased more of the goods and services that they had once either produced or done without.[30] Whites followed in the tradition of their antebellum ancestors, attracted by what Daniel Horowitz calls "market-oriented cultural commodities," and ended up behaving as if they believed gentility could be purchased and possessed. Horowitz thinks that this occurred as the "rural middle class tried to validate its achievement and aspirations through additional artifacts."[31] This was especially true of Newman. Whether or not Page fell into this category is difficult to ascertain. His 1873 declaration of bankruptcy reflected his crippled ability to purchase. He simply ran out of money and credit.

Patterns

This community's black males and black women with families appear to have followed Newman's pattern a generation or two later. The women who equated fancy table wear with sophistication, and the fine things that a single woman had who was still living under her father's roof, seem to be the exception to this trend.

In other New South communities, whites and blacks with little or no economic resources looked on, admired what money could buy, and bought things as their discretionary incomes allowed. They watched as middle-class whites bought land and then built homes. The purchase of durable goods usually preceded the purchase of luxury items. Anxious to participate in consumer society, poor whites and blacks altered the southern patterns of consumption. Small items for special days often became the first items they could afford to buy. Bronner says that even the poorest rural southerner bought firecrackers and explosive torpedoes that they "deemed essential to a festive Christmas."[32] If blacks in this community did this, the evidence does not remain in documents or oral histories.

Persons with little money to spend, but with keen desires, were assisted locally and nationally in their quest to consume. During the 1880s, the United States Mint coined the nickel for the first time. Many items had become available for as little as a few cents. Many of these inexpensive items were found in country stores such as West's and Hall's, local places where you could buy just about anything. Rural merchants led by example, often buying gadgets for themselves and showing them off to anyone who would look. Merchants demonstrated in their own lives how much enjoyment the novelty of things could bring. Drummers walked the countryside promoting products with posters and painted signs. They helped local merchants because their contacts with the public made them financial consultants, economic forecasters, market analysts, and advertising experts.[33] Belmont and Caryswood workers often saw peddlers walking down the roads to their homes. These peddlers, often remembered as gypsies, regularly traveled through this community selling some items and, it was believed by some, stealing others. Portraits of household heads imprinted on round metal plates hung in many a family front room thanks to other merchants who roamed the countryside talking folks into standing alone or with other "serious faces" and having their images captured.

On a national level, mail-order catalogs became steady, strong, and constant competitors for the buyer's attention. In this community, however, there is little evidence that this is the case. Illiteracy would have been a stumbling block for many. Newman does not cite one instance in which he shared or ordered something from a catalog for any of his workers, black or white. In other places, the Haynes-Cooper catalog was consulted so often for advice concerning crops it became known as the Farmer's Bible. Montgomery Ward in 1872 and Richard Sears in 1889 issued semiannual publications describing, in tempting ways, all kinds of things. The Farmer's Wish Book became a reader, textbook, and encyclopedia in many rural schoolhouses.[34] There is no evidence that blacks in this community looked to catalogs as providers of goods until the late 1920s. It appears that blacks did not become catalog users during this period for three reasons (besides illiteracy): First of all, they could readily obtain goods from Page and Newman. Second, they had access to general stores and peddlers. Third, their incomes did not permit expenditures beyond the food, shelter, and clothing they obtained locally.

Thus the experiences of blacks working at Caryswood and Belmont do not fall into the larger patterns that Ransom and Sutch suggest occurred elsewhere in the New South. But what these African Americans experienced was similar in some ways to blacks living elsewhere at this time.

There is evidence that Caryswood and Belmont workers did create a group economy which was tied very closely to kinship. As was discussed earlier, interpersonal relationships became evident when men, women, and children paid each other's accounts and bought items for each other. A case study of African American life in one Deep South community further confirms that consumerism and culture linked hands and that blacks in this community did share experiences with freed people elsewhere. In "Gotta Mind to Move, a Mind to Settle Down," Sydney Nathans discusses the economic, social, and political aftermaths of slavery in the Mississippi Cotton Delta. Nathans reveals that this one particular community experienced three different periods of racial relationships between 1865 and 1915. The first period, 1865–1885, represented a standoff. In trying to cope with the challenges of emancipation, white plantation owners and black farmhands waged battles for the limited available resources. Whites learned not to raise their voices when speaking to potential workers and blacks sharpened their skills in dealing with whites. Blacks "got out of the way of whites," often preferring to live away from them in wilderness areas.

African Americans were said to have "got back there among the wolves," opting to live with wild animals rather than white men.[35] In the Caryswood and Belmont community, however, census records, journals, and account books proclaim that blacks and whites stayed on the same farms after the Civil War. Oral histories confirm that all that separated the races in most cases was a yard, stream, or hill.

Many blacks outside of this community became mail-order catalog users. They preferred not to deal with local merchants, who often appeared angered about their choices and purchases. When not buying from catalogs, they bought items from each other, creating what

Nathans calls a "group economy." There were numerous occasions when Caryswood and Belmont blacks shared and traded with each other, as well. These instances were often witnessed by James Newman, who wrote them down.

During the second and third periods that Nathans describes, 1885–1915, plantation owners gained the upper hand. Blacks tried but could not remain independent of white landholders because they did not have the resources to secure their independence and/or gain elevated powerful positions in the community. Nathans discloses that it was only after blacks realized that their economic status was not going to change that they changed their buying patterns. He asserts, "for Delta and Black Belt plantation workers, as for industrial workers in the urban North, acquisition of personal objects became an alternative to blocked social ascent."[36] This appears to have been true in the Caryswood and Belmont community, but only in a very limited sense, perhaps because land was obtainable. Single women purchased more personal objects than those with other responsibilities.

Joe A. Mobley's study of Princeville, North Carolina, analyzes another black community during this same time period and allows for another comparison of this community's experiences with those elsewhere. Mobley's findings show that when blacks were in the majority, black consumerism was constructed very differently than white consumerism or black consumerism as it existed within biracial communities.[37] It appears that Caryswood and Belmont laborers more closely resembled this all-black community than biracial communities that have been explored elsewhere.

Princeville was different in ways other than its racial makeup. Instead of seeking employment in agricultural occupations, blacks turned to industrialization for work to earn a living. Princeville's nearness to Tarboro, North Carolina, allowed blacks to find employment as day laborers, carpenters, brick masons, painters, seamstresses, nurses, cooks, draymen, and mattress makers.

The first purchases of African Americans living in Princeville were not gadgets and toy-like objects. Blacks saved their incomes and purchased inexpensive parcels of land that area whites did not want. They then spent money building houses.[38] This was not true in the community studied in this book. Here, people purchased land but did not spend a lot of money putting a house on it. Many still lived in cabins until the middle of the twentieth century. Oral histories often mention how most homes had holes in the walls big enough to see through.

While the first Princeville homes were described as huts, most people were able to build more substantial second homes called saddle-bag houses, so named because of their center halls and two side rooms. The town of Princeville became known as the city of flowers because every dwelling was well kept and covered with flowering vines.[39] African American Caryswood, and Belmont workers grew flowers in yards of homes that they owned.

In Princeville, unlike other black communities, commercialism and consumption seemed to come before religion. This was not the case in this community. The people in and around Belmont and Caryswood, like others across the New South, established churches before many of them purchased their own land, as soon as possible after emancipation. The people of Princeville did not have their own preacher or church until after 1880.[40]

Charles E. Orser's anthropological investigations of a South Carolina Piedmont plantation provides yet another example of black experience which does not parallel what took place in this community. Orser states that freed mens' diets reflect increased portions of meat, and that the first purchases of freedman "mirrored those of slaves" and included "beads, shoe buckles, buttons and smoking pipes."[41] His findings could very well be restricted by the nature of his research. Beads, buckles, buttons, and pipes can be dug up after eighty years, while cloth usually deteriorates in this much time.

Orser does, however, forge a connection between freedom and African American household material culture. He discloses that the homes of free people had more furniture and of a greater variety. Mattresses had been rare in slave cabins. They became more plentiful in the dwellings of free blacks, as they came to represent upward mobility and progress after emancipation. Orser quotes a descendant of the community he studied as saying, "Every time you moved up in the world, you got a better mattress."[42] This finding gives meaning to the presence of the one full-time mattress maker who lived in Princeville in 1880. The mattress maker's work stood for more than just making mattresses; he was producing a luxury that people used as a barometer of their success.

Many of the items such as chairs were homemade, "with bottoms of rye splits, oak splits or cane. The preferred ones were made of rye splits."[43] Orser's observations are in keeping with Caryswood and Belmont documentary evidence and the oral record. When people moved, it often took a number of wagon loads to cart away their household goods. Wilson Morris, a Belmont worker who never achieved economic stability, nonetheless acquired enough belongings to require two oxen to pull the wagon on his moving day to Belmont in 1882. Under the personal property section on the census record, however, there was seldom anything of value claimed. No person in this community left a will in the nineteenth century.

In settings where racial discrimination existed, African Americans developed different purchasing patterns tied to their enslaved past and present conditions. Politics in the New South adjudicated how much blacks earned and what they were able to purchase. This was true for the entire southern region, as studies of the Deep and Upper South confirm.

Given limited purchasing opportunities and incomes, blacks consumed what became important to them because of their culture. For example, because meat had been so severely restricted during enslavement, they desired and added large portions of meat to their diets–if, and only if, they had the earning power to do so. Blacks were often shadows of the white people whose secondhand clothes they wore. Many a woman walked around in Pattie Newman's discarded dresses and many a man in James Newman's worn pants. And while some blacks were satisfied with beads and trinkets, others, such as the ones in this community, were not pacified by childlike trinkets or toys. Common sense wedded practicalities and necessity, making futile purchases rare.

Princeville blacks demonstrated that given the opportunity and income, blacks would have kept the same purchasing patterns as whites. This is in agreement with what took place here. Blacks wanted to be a part of the system. While blacks and poor whites belonged to the same economic class, their discretionary income was not the determining factor in the kinds of items they purchased. Items were consumed because of what they represented in slavery and came to mean in freedom. Like other groups, such as poor rural whites and new Jewish immigrants, blacks used consumerism to Americanize themselves, seeking to transfer the meanings of things onto images of themselves.

5. Spoken Words

Even in a small community made up of a network of plantations, there were different worlds, each of them filled with words.
Images of a school house and a family group feature the members
of two of the worlds within this community. A few months before
he died in 1929, William Wade appeared to be the picture of
health as a laughing boy sitting with his classmates. His was the
second generation to have a public school to attend in Buckingham County, Virginia.

Fatherless Van Woodson children assembled in the front yard
of their family home before a camera in the early 1930s, their
sober expressions suggesting the hardships they faced during the
lean years of the Depression. While silent in this image, their
words continue to fill the mornings, noons, and nights of their
generation and the generations that have followed.

The granddaughter of slaves stands outside her own garden
gate, tilts her head back so that all that she sees is the sky. One of
her many granddaughters, practiced at duplicating the elder's
every movement, does the same.

"Old folks used to say that the sky will tell you if or not the
rain is going to come. All you have to do is look and the answer is
there. You must suppose that the sky is a piece of cloth. If you can
find a piece of clear sky–a cloudless piece–big enough to fashion a
pair of men's trousers from, then that means that no rain is going
to come your way. This is a fact. It's always good to keep a piece
of your life clear, without clouds–trouble. Keep it with some big
patches of clearing in it–peace. Then trouble can't take over.
Things won't shower down on you all at once. Old folks told me
that and I'm telling it to you. Just you remember."

The child understands skies and rain. She does not yet understand trouble. But she does as she is told and from then on remembered how to foretell a rainstorm and how to keep trouble
from taking over a life.[1]

Jones School No. 8, Buckingham County, Virginia, 1929
FRONT ROW, LEFT TO RIGHT: *Turner Taylor, Aubrey Spuggen Harris, Daniel Benjamin Tyree, Robert Easter Carter, John William Wade, Archer Gilbert Booker, Lucy Florence Carter, Ethel Marie Scruggs, Edith Priscilla Woodson, Martha Anne Booker, Lucy Naomi Harris, Elizabeth Tyree, Russell Delaney Harris, John Harris.* MIDDLE ROW, LEFT TO RIGHT: *Alfred Lee Harris, Daisy Bell Carter, Mr. Joseph Wesley White (teacher), Dan Henderson Wade, Hazel Ayers, Pearl Scruggs, Betty Sears, Gracie Scruggs, Louise Nannie Wade, Fanny Doretha Woodson, James Sears, Cassie Scruggs, Martha Ann Scruggs, Joseph Lloyd Harris, Julia Branch.*

Van and Mary Woodson's youngest children
LEFT TO RIGHT: *John, Walker, Edith, Van (Stokes), James, and Fanny Woodson (seated), April 1932.*

This chapter focuses on the outward actions of generations who made ways for themselves against life's circumstances. The census records, journals, account books, and receipts combined with family oral histories provide evidence of agency and action; sayings, anecdotes, and stories provide even more. These words, always spoken, never written down, most often do not reference occasions of which the world outside of this community took note. Rather, they provide glances at motivations, opinions, and values of a people who did not write down what directed them to do the things that they did. According to Paul Thompson, the importance of these words do not rest upon their "adherence to facts but rather in their divergence from them where imagination, symbolism and desire break in."[2] They are admittance to thoughts and mind-sets of the people who worked Caryswood and Belmont fields before, during, and after the Civil War.

My daughter, as the hearer of these stories and the reader of century-old documents, is a reluctant visitor to places in this book. The people have come alive for her. She imagines that, like the roads that lead to the old home places and plantations, the people are still there–waiting to whisper to her in the winter winds, creak the floor boards of old houses in the spring, or climb up ladders to cabin and barn lofts. Her memories are to blame. Selectively she has drawn on what remains–the documents, the stories, and the photographs–constructing a reality where the people are so vivid they do not stand still. They repeat the stories she has heard so many times, again and again in what is now her present. From the collective memories of others she has fashioned her own. Her history, like all histories, is the residue of what is left–that which has not been thrown away, lost, or forgotten.

These words, a saying or phrase here and a story there, were never intended to see the light of any day beyond the speaker's voice and their intended audience. And it is for this reason that they are so useful. These spoken words often contradicted the socially acceptable answers to questions, bestowing meaning to events best thought left alone. When asked, for example, if people ever talked about Africa, immediate answers were always "No." The stories themselves prove differently. An eighty-two-year-old woman, who had answered with a negative, explained how her own grandmother said that she had come to Virginia during slavery times when she was a baby, "from across the water, from the old country, in her mother's apron. Her mother had told her not to cry, not to make a sound and she did not."[3] This recollection of the middle passage survived not because it linked to Africa, but because it provided an example of a child, even as an infant, exercising exceptional restraint to obey an elder.

In another interview, Africa proved to be a place to which a person just walked off to, never to return. One of Newman's workers (and my paternal great-grandfather), Charles Swann, left home one morning forever.

One of his son's families tells the story that he went back to Africa, and that is why he was never heard from again. In this scenario, Africa is revealed as a place very isolated from home, even antithetical to home.[4]

The Civil War was another topic people did not wish to discuss, but which was, nevertheless, a part of the community's frame of reference. Without exception when informants were asked, "Did you ever hear what happened during the Civil War?" each informant again answered no. It was the community's figures of speech and not its stories, however, in this instance which provided the true answer of the war's impact. Over 130 years after any Confederate soldier wore a uniform in the line of service, this community's descendants still call a person "reb-ish" if they displayed selfish or thoughtless behavior toward a black person. And each time someone uses the expression, and they frequently do, "as long as Grant hung around Richmond" to measure an extended time period, it is evident that the community knew of the North's determined military campaigns and how its battles influenced their historical status.

It was the lyrics to a single song which hinted at gender relations and work responsibilities following emancipation. When asked if they remembered or knew anything about how men and women behaved during courtship, all men and women said no, that they never talked about such things with old folks. I did recall one song that my father sang whenever he was particularly happy, and asked informants if they were familiar with the words. They were. Only three lines comprised the song as it was sung in this community: "Hey, little girl if you were mine / You wouldn't do nothing but wash and iron. / Whoa! whoa!"[5]

It appears that this song was often sung by young men as they approached the homes of women they were courting. Suitors bellowed out these lyrics. The last line was often followed by hearty laughter. The song was never actually sung in the woman's presence, but was a way of letting her know that should she decide to marry the man who sought her out, she would not have to do field work or work in anyone's kitchen except her own.

Short phrases and lyrics slip into a community's language, with their own singular definitions, anecdotes, and stories. People pass on stories for reasons, usually having to do with identity and safety or survival. Stories that convey identity detail individual parentage and family ancestry dating back to one person or a specific place. In some instances, identity stories connect groups to a specific place or set of characteristics. Identity stories for the descendants of Page and Newman workers often made clear that the "old people worked real hard," "never bothered anybody," and "all knew how to pray." Those people differed from others who "would always tell a lie," "cut you as quick as they would look at you," or "swear all over the table."

Safety and survival stories were and are told to keep people alive. They permitted children and young people to learn from the mistakes of others, and to gain the knowledge needed to survive and have a healthy, less troublesome, life. Safety and survival stories often had elders or ancestors as their subjects. Neighbors and "folks everybody knew" frequently became examples–good and bad ones. One man, a Caryswood worker Ed Trent, came to represent someone who was not a hard worker. Most stories identified him as "someone who would not work in a pie shop."

Identity stories were shared at mileposts in a person's life: when you become an adult, or left home, or got married, or when there was a birth or a death in the family or community. Safety and survival stories are unlimited by circumstance. They are told whenever an occasion arises and are repeated again and again. Because actual life and well-being are dependent on knowing these stories, they cannot be told too often.

All stories, no matter what their type, have "inside and outside" meanings. In the Emancipation Yard story, slaveholder Edward T. Page summoned together all of the people he held, to announce the North's Civil War victory and the end of slavery. The outside meaning, for example, is "this is how we found out about freedom." The inside meaning is more complex and full. The inside passes on information about the nature of slaveholders:in this case they are revealed as driving hard bargains. The inside also emphasizes that the family survived slavery as a family unit which lived in a larger slave community. Also included are the inside messages that as a people they know where they came from before freedom (the family has a long history), and that freedom brought choices that were not always easy ones to make but choices nevertheless.

Charlotte Linde believes that it is not necessary to study a person's entire life, or every word that is spoken, in order to see the coherence of what that person's life entailed or that for which it stood.[6] This is the same for a people. The sayings and stories explored here do not include every story told by the original members of this community or their descendants. They are a collection of stories told repeatedly to the gatherer over the full course of her life.

Some stories were told to others of her generation and then passed on to her, such as the one about the clear patch of sky. Some were a part of every evening's hours–grown folks' talk. Still others came to light in the course of asking two questions for this research: "What did they say?" and "What did they do?" In a community where a person's word was considered his or her bond, it was these two questions that unlocked the gates to a flood of stories. "What did they say?" and "What did they do?" became self-defining questions, letting people offer their interpretation of their ancestors' influence on the community's history and culture.[7]

The stories that follow are what Ralph Ellison termed the first drawings of a group's character, their oral folklore.[8] They are offered here in the order in which they would have taken place. Each is given in as near to the way as it was told as possible.

IN HER APRON

Grandma Juda Ann said that she was brought over here, from the old country, across the water in a big boat. She said that her mother hid her in her apron while they were on board that boat and told her not to cry. She did not.

Juda Ann Monroe Swann is described as a small, red-skinned woman who worked all of the time, humming all the while. She is said to have awakened each morning "way before day, at 4 or 4:30," at which time she would pray and sing. While it seems that it is very likely that she came to Virginia from some place within the

United States and not from the "old country," her descendants all believe that she came from Africa. Her strong work ethic and habit of singing constantly lent credence to this belief.⁹

IN THE HOUSE

Grandpa Matt was a tiny boy when they first took him in the house. I bet he wasn't more than this tall. Took him in there to nurse Miss Betsy after her baby died and her milk wouldn't dry up. At first, would just send for him in the day, one or two times. Then he started staying in there at night during the War, when Mr. Page was off fighting. He stayed in there, though, until he was a grown man, nursing Miss Betsy, long after her dead baby would have been almost grown, had it lived. Yes, indeed, kept Grandpa Matt in that house, nursing that white woman's breast till he was grown enough to get married and just stopped going. Miss Betsy would still send for him sometimes but he wouldn't go. Folks just didn't talk about it. That's all.

Matthew Wade's presence and duties in the Caryswood Plantation house were explained by women on both sides of the color line. Edith Woodson Swann said that she had been told by her mother, Mary Wade Woodson (Matthew Wade's daughter), that Matthew had been used to suckle milk from the plantation mistress's breast when he was an infant, and that the practice continued for years, ending when he was a grown man and refused to engage in what had long since become a sexual practice. The plantation mistress's granddaughter, Elizabeth Page Trent Bird (1903–1993), acknowledged that Wade had, in fact, slept in the Caryswood Plantation house but said that he had done so because her grandfather Edward T. Page was away fighting for the Confederacy, leaving the house and the women and children unprotected. Wade, she said, "slept in the house to protect everybody from the Yankees." According to census records, Matthew Wade was born in either 1863 or 1865. The Page family Bible records the birth date of a child, Mary C. Page, in 1861. There is no death date listed for this child. Edward and Elizabeth

C. N. Page did not record any children born to them during the en-
suing Civil War years. It is possible that Matthew Wade's presence
in the household was associated with the death of a Page child, per-
haps Mary C. Page. Evidence of Wade's birth renders the white de-
scendant's explanation for Wade's presence in the home implausible.
As an infant, Wade could not have protected the household against
anyone.[10]

Suit Yourself

They said that Old Man Page called all of them out into the
front yard over at Caryswood. Told them that the war was
over and that they were free. Said that they could leave or
they could stay. Just had to suit themselves.

Said that he would give them all, a family apiece, one cast-
iron pot or skillet. If they left they could take that with them.
But that was all that they could take, that pot. Said that everything else they would have to leave behind cause it was his.

They could go or they could stay on to work for him as
they had before. He would pay them for their days, and they
would pay him for what they got off him. They could suit
themselves. Some folks left, but we stayed on.

William Howard Woodson, the oldest child of Van and Mary Wade
Woodson, is the only person who tells this story in the family. Per-
haps it fell to him, as the oldest male child, to pass on this story to
other family members. Perhaps he remembered the story and took
ownership of it because he knew some of the people who stood in that
yard. His paternal grandmother, Nannie Peaks Woodson, would
have been a toddler probably standing close to her mother Maria
and grandmother. His maternal great-grandfather, Jerry Wade,
would have been a youngster probably standing near his father
Moses and brothers Van and Sam. All of the people that Woodson
knew who stood in that yard would have worked for Page and
Newman at Caryswood or Belmont.[11]

Uncle Caesar and the Branches

Uncle Caesar never pretended to be anything other than a conjurer. You sure wouldn't find him in any church of no form or fashion. Every spring he would go round to folk's places and say that for a fee he would break one branch on that person's land and nothing would die the whole year. He'd say, "Now don't you hire me unless you want your crops to grow, cause if I break that branch, everything on this here land is going to keep on growing until first frost and maybe some after that."

Uncle Caesar made lots of money doing that. Don't know what he did with it all. Didn't spend it on clothes that's for sure, dressed in rags, all over himself—one rag right on top of the other—like he always was.

Over the course of his life, Caesar Tyree, a Belmont worker, earned a solid reputation as a conjurer in the black community. The son of Daniel and Virginia Tyree, he grew up in a household with others who practiced the art, passing knowledge and skills generationally. The descendants of one of Tyree's neighbors and another Belmont worker, Jordan Brown, shared this story. Royal Brown (1888–1972), Jordan Brown's son, shared this story with his son George Jordan Brown (1935–). Royal Brown said that his father had paid for Tyree's services and that it had been money well spent.[12]

Dyin' Grace This Mornin'

Two barefooted children, a six-year-old brother and his younger sister, had been sent to the spring for a bucket of water. They did not try to walk down the steep slope to the place where they would draw the water, it was so much fun just letting the hill pull them head over heel to the bottom of it. Once there, even before their giggles were gone, they could hear the shouts, "I done got the dyin' grace this mornin' . . . the dyin' grace this mornin'."

Unaware of what the dying grace was but knowing the

voice and where the shout came from, they followed the path to the cabin door of their great-grandfather, Jerry Wade. From outside the door they saw a sight, unbelievable even to their young eyes. There was Grandpa Jer standing on his own two legs, something they had seldom in their lifetime seen him do. And not only was he standing, he was walking, albeit with some difficulty, but walking nevertheless, all around his cabin, his pet pig following his every step.

"Go tell your pa and your ma that I done got the dyin' grace this morning and that I goin' on home now!" Without having to be told twice, the two youngsters lit off. They took the path back to the spring, jumped over the bucket that they had left there, and half fell half flew up the hill to their parents' home. "Come quick, Great Grandpa Jer said he got the grace and is goin' this mornin'."

Without a word, their father ran from the house, taking the same path to the old man's quarter. Death met them at the door. On the floor beside the old man lay the pig, both dead and resting in the mixture of blood and fluid that had been freed from the Jer's tight dropsied legs at long last.

The children were turned away. They didn't get to see any more. They would always remember what they had seen and the whispers that followed. Their old Great-Grandpa, born during slavery times, had had a vision and blessing from God, on the morning of his death day. The dying grace, he called it. His only companion, an old hog, with whom he had shared his last years and who was considered too dear to eat, had followed him quickly to the other side, not wanting to stay here without the one who had protected and loved him enough to spare and feed his life.

Ethel Woodson Bolden told this story about her great-grandfather's, Jerry Wade's, death. Wade worked for Newman and was the father of Matthew and Polly Wade.[13]

The outside message of story falls into the identity category. It places the family within a framework of Christian believers. Its inside message shares how things were and what was important. Chil-

dren had fun even while doing chores. Children began contributing to the family's well-being at an early age by bringing wood for the stove and fireplace and toting water. A former enslaved man had reached a measure of success by having a hog that he did not have to kill. Times since slavery had not been without some measure of success. Children should listen to adults and do as they are told.

JUST WALKED OFF

They said that they don't know what happened to Mr. Charles Swann. They say that he left home one morning and just walked off. Never did come back home. Some say he went back to Africa, and came back for a visit one time and bought some hats back and hung them in the hall on the hook, but we never saw him or those hats. He just walked off.[14]

While courthouse documents suggest that Mr. Charles Swann's ambition made him risk his fortune on a tobacco crop which did not pan out, the family does not let the possibility of failure enter into its memory of him. To consider that Swann had gone to jail for his crime of wanting land, or had become entrapped in peonage, was too hard a reality to face. As a former slave and family patriarch, such a message would have proved to be too daunting to those who followed. Africa appears to be a place far away, a place from which goods could be gotten and kept by family members. The idea that he returned with material and tangible goods and then left again gave the message that he was not dead or unable to return home. This story satisfies the trauma surrounding his disappearance by twisting reality to a good end.

TURKEY IN THE POT

Sometimes, white folks get mad when you have more than they do, everybody knows this. One time two sons saw a turkey in the woods that was too big and too fine *not* to kill. With one shot, they plugged the bird, right between the eyes. He was so big they had to drag him off the white man's place where they had trespassed to kill him. It didn't take much for the white man to follow the hunters' trail with turkey in tow back to the cabin where they lived with their parents and old Grandma, born during slavery times. But white men aren't trackers, so they had to follow their noses to the place where their prize bird had been taken.

When the boys came home with the turkey, Grandma Juda Ann knew just what to do. It was no problem for her that the bird was too big for any of the pots in the house. With the assistance of her son, his wife, and their children, they quickly dressed the turkey—everyone had to help. Some picked feathers, while others prepared the big kettle used for making soap and others built a cooking fire close to the wood pile. It didn't take long for the strong aroma of the cooking bird to fill the countryside.

When the white man from whose land the bird had been taken came into sight, Grandma Juda told everyone to mind themselves and let her talk. She greeted the white man with a nod and continued to stir the pot. "What you got there Aunt Juda, in that there pot? It sure smells good."

"I here making soap today, Mr. L. Making soap for the wintertime."

"Doesn't smell like soap. Smells like fresh turkey cookin' over an open fire to me."

"Ah. Don't smell like fresh turkey to me. Smell just like soap cooking in my pot, same as it always do."

With that, the white man frowned, shook his head and walked away saying, "Enjoy your soap, Aunt Juda."

"I expects that I will," replied the old woman, who never stopped stirring.

This incident took place in the 1920s after Juda Ann Swann's husband had "walked off from home forever." She was living in the home of her oldest son John and his wife Olivia Jane Tyree Swann. Mattie Pearl Swann Wade Bethea tells this story, which falls into both the identity and safety and survival categories. Hearers of this story are encouraged to do as they are told by this old grandmother who came from Africa. Holding your tongue, and sticking to the same story, could keep you fed and alive.[15]

REAL MEAN BACK THEN

They say that Uncle Benny was talking to this white woman, this white man's daughter, and the white man came to the house to see Benny about it. Say he got after Uncle Benny real bad and Uncle Benny ran up the ladder to the loft and the man was after him so bad, he jumped out the window and broke his leg real bad. Say the white man didn't do nothin' to him after that–he just went off home, but he told the doctors and them not to set Uncle Benny's leg. Uncle Benny's leg never did set right. Those bones would break through his skin and work their way out. Uncle Benny saved them in a matchbox. Said that he wanted to go to heaven and knew that he couldn't get in without all his bones, so he kept them in a matchbox and said he wanted to be buried with them. He never did walk right after that.

This story concerning Benjamin Woodson was told by male and female descendants of one of his brothers, Van Woodson, and one of his sisters, Lillian Woodson Winn. It appears to function as safety-survival story warning that whites could be "real mean" and that it could be dangerous to talk to white women. Van Woodson's sons and daughters declare that they had seen the match box containing their uncle's bones. They believed that he was buried with them. In an oral history interview, one of Lillian Woodson Winn's daughters shared the story of how Woodson's leg was injured and confirmed that it never did heal right. She, too, saw the box in which he kept his bones. She added that her uncle had not been buried with them, however. Before he died, Woodson attempted to rid his bed of chiggers by burning sulfur inside the house. Bed linens caught fire, consuming many of his belongings, including the matchbox filled with his bones. Wood stated that Woodson was distressed "by his bones getting to heaven before he did." As the person who made Woodson's funeral arrangements several years later, she was sure that he was not buried with a matchbox. "They [the bones] were already gone on," she said.[16]

COUSIN POLLY

As sixty-year-old Polly Wade lay on her deathbed, she asked for a few crackers, so that she might eat them and not die hungry. Born in 1868, the child of former slaves, too many of her days had been marred by a keen want for food. Surrounded by family, most standing cramped in her two-room cabin, she tried to eat just one more time–for all of the times she had wanted to but couldn't. She died with her mouth full.[17]

FRIED CHICKEN, A FEW PEAS, AND SOME ROLLS

The two sisters decided that even though they had never gotten enough to eat of their favorite foods, there was something they could do, something about this very thing. They would wait until their mother left one day, to go off to the plantation where she worked, and cook all of the foods they loved but had never gotten enough of because they were two girls in a family with seven brothers who always ate first, taking the best parts of the chicken, just about all of the greens, and most of the peas.

By the time their mother's back had disappeared down the path leading to the Caryswood plantation, they were at the stove readying the pots. They would cook a meal of fried chicken, fresh green peas, and hot rolls. It didn't look like too much flour at first because they knew they wanted to make lots of rolls. They would smother and stuff some of the rolls with butter, others they would eat plain. They had seen their mother put down rolls many times and knew, or so they thought, how much of each ingredient to use including their mother's precious yeast.

Three chickens should be enough for them. After all, they had no intention of eating the parts usually left to them, the backs, necks, and wings. They planned to have as many thighs, drum sticks, and breasts as they could eat.

They filled a roaster with the green peas that they picked from their mother's garden. They would cook down, wouldn't they?

The rising bread gave the first hint of trouble. It was slowly but surely taking over the kitchen table. Just as soon as they wiped the table clean of the bubbling mask, it would grow over the sides of the bowl onto the table and then to the floor. They would have to take it outside. That would slow it down. Outside didn't help. They would have to divide it and bury some of it in the ground, maybe two holes would be better since there was so much of it. In a short time, bread dough was growing out of two holes in the ground. They would have to find a way to cover it up after they cleaned up the peas that instead of cooking down in the pot, were multiplying. A big problem.

They floured the freshly cooked chicken and decided to forgo the lard they usually cooked it in for a couple of large pints of butter. It would taste better cooked in all butter instead of the little they had seen their mother use. They found out that it certainly smelled better too, if that was possible, but it also burned faster. They would throw away the pieces that "got too brown."

Their meal was a memorable one. They got enough to eat—in fact they ate too much. Both had a hard time looking at green peas for a long time after that. And one doesn't care too much for fried chicken even today. Their mother missed the flour but never found the spots where it grew out of the ground on that one afternoon.

The two sisters are Van (1882–1932) and Mary Wade Woodson's (1888–1968) second and third daughters, Fanny Woodson Gregory (1918–1982) and Edith Woodson Swann (1920–1995).[18]

They Won't Do You No Harm

We could hear him crying long ways before we got to their place. William, you see, was real sick—real poorly. Robert and us went in there to see about him. We were on our way to school. There he was, laying up there in bed with snakes hanging down from the wall, all over that bed's headboard. Robert, he turned and ran home for his gun. Aunt Lou said, "Oh, don't you all worry none, those snakes ain't going to hurt him. Just leave them be."

In no time Robert was back with his gun and shot one of those snakes. Aunt Lou just about had a fit. She was so mad. William, he died a short time later, and Robert, he wasn't no more good to himself after that. He was left for dead on a battlefield in World War II but he didn't die. And then this growth grew out of his jaw and that killed him when he was right in the middle of being a man. I felt his hands at the hospital before he died and they were so cold. I knew he was going. Aunt Lou told him not to kill that snake, to leave those snakes alone.

Three of Van and Mary Wade Woodson's children, Robert (1915–1965), Fanny (1918–1982) and Edith (1920–1995) responded to their cousin William Wade's cries. William Wade (1920–1929) was the oldest child and the only son of John and Louise Tyree Wade. John Wade was the son of Matthew and Martha Wade and a younger brother of Mary Wade Woodson. Louise Tyree Wade grew up in a household of conjurers headed by Caesar Tyree's brother John and his wife Zenobia Booker Tyree. Louise Tyree Wade, as did one of her sisters Lou, had a reputation of being able to work roots. Olivia Jane Tyree Swann, another sister, is said not to have participated in their practices.[19]

CAN'T DO NOTHIN' WITH UNCLE LEWIS

It was in the last of October 1939, and they had been fixing for that day for weeks. Most everybody around would be at the wedding which would take place in the front yard. The table was set for people to come inside and eat after the ceremony. Uncle Lewis came in and started cutting up as always. "You all think that you've set a nice table. Looks like a white

Linwood and Edith Woodson Swann with wedding guests, 1939

folks table to me," assessed Uncle Lewis. "Yes this looks just like a white folks table to me."

Without saying another word, Uncle Lewis, who everyone by this time suspected had had a taste too much, turned over a big bowl of peas onto the tablecloth and proceeded to eat them directly from the table just like a pig. The women standing around were too angry to speak. When Uncle Lewis finished "his meal" he wiped his mouth on the tablecloth and left. The women removed and replaced the tablecloth and set the table again, all the while saying, "You can't do nothin' with Uncle Lewis."

The Uncle Lewis in this story is Lewis Morris, the son of longtime Belmont worker, Alexander Morris, and himself a Belmont and a Caryswood field hand. He worked at both Caryswood and Belmont and was the first person in the Wade family to purchase land. The women who watched his antics and cleaned up the table were his sister, "Sis" Annie Morris, and his nieces, Charlotte Morris and Mary Wade Woodson; Mary's daughter Edith Woodson was about to marry J. Linwood Swann, the son of John and Olivia Jane Tyree Swann, in October 1939. This story serves an identity function. It conveys that there was a person in the family who did not respect white people's ways. Family members recognized Lewis Morris as having attained economic success and security by saving enough money to purchase land.[20]

These stories, most of them occurring after 1865, function in ways similar to slave narratives. They do more than report events. By their presence, their survival, they weigh themselves as being instances too important to be forgotten. They talk back to stereotypes by denying portrayals of rural freed people and their descendants as lazy, backwards, complacent, and ignorant. The themes are also in keeping with those put forward by slave narratives. The securing and consumption of food is present in almost half of these stories. The second-oldest story mentions being given an empty pot and not being given any food to put in it. The two death-day stories (Dyin' Grace and Cousin Polly) involve the lack of food and the presence of a hog, the primary source of meat for most blacks. Grandma Juda Ann's cooking in the front yard and the sisters' attempt to create the perfect meal for themselves are additional examples. Each of these stories highlights the agency people exercised to make their lives better. Hunters provided food for the table because they were skilled, had good eyes, and knew what to do.

The dependence children had on adults and the importance of the family unit is emphasized in just as many stories. Baby Juda Ann, brought to Virginia as a helpless infant, could only do as she was told. Grandpa Matt, ordered into the plantation house to nurse his white mistress, had to go and do whatever he was told. Sick William, who could only cry out to keep the snakes away which hung down over his bed, was at his mother's mercy. The sisters, whose judgment and lack of experience ill-prepared them to cook a meal in their mother's absence, illustrated the wasteful follies of youth.

According to these stories, whites were not at the center of the lives of these African Americans. All of the stories are about blacks, only one-third of them have white characters. The whites who are mentioned are not heroes or problem-solvers. In the emancipation story a white man, in the teller's opinion, drives a hard, and unfair, bargain. The white man who got after Uncle Benny real hard is said to have showed him a dirty turn by making sure that he would not receive medical care for his leg. Mr. L who followed his nose to Grandma Juda Ann's front yard was no match for her. While the plantation mistress solved her own problem, she created an uncomfortable situation for Grandpa Matt who did not want to be sexually intimate with her during his youth and early adulthood. From these instances, it appears that blacks regarded whites as selfish, hardhearted, and unwilling to consider the black person's well-being.

These stories convey forward-thinking, never-give-up attitudes. Polly Wade's story fostered the idea that it is never too late to do something about your circumstance. Uncle Caesar could go up against nature and win. As a powerful black man, like Lewis Morris, he was successful. Grandma Juda Ann kept her story straight, not letting anyone tell her how to handle her situation.

These were the messages that were passed on. These were the messages that all were to keep.

6. A Coming Together

✿ The earliest photograph of Ethel Beulah Woodson Bolden captures her as a toddler, out of her mother's arms and standing with three generations of her family in front of a slave cabin, someone's family home.

Nearly twenty years later, the illness of her father sent her off alone to Richmond, where she was photographed as a lone person in a foreign but fancy studio.

It all came to this. Edward T. Page did not live to see the twentieth century, and James Moore Newman did not live beyond the first few months of it. Many of their workers did.

Page's family buried him in the family's plot a hundred yards and a pathway off the Caryswood house side-entrance yard. His gravestone gives only his name and Civil War Regiment—almost as if nothing else mattered in his life.[1] No one knows the location of Newman's final resting place. His estate papers provide the details of his demise and death. Two white men, Frank Barker and Newman's nephew, each sat with him five nights, waiting with him for wellness or death to come. Wellness did not come, and Caesar Tyree, the only field hand Newman employed at the time, saw his brother Jacob dig Newman's grave, after undertaker J. D. Harris had prepared the body for burial.[2] The last ten days of Newman's life were not characteristic of his final months. Diary entries made the first three months of this century claim what must have been a lonely and quiet time in the seventy-eight-year-old man's life. He noted the work activities of his cook Puss Randolph, sometimes called on to help field laborer Caesar Tyree haul chip manure and hay, weigh millet, move sorghum, and go off looking for pigs. Day after day, Newman said that he was "at home unwell," "sick in the house," "very weak and sick [to his] stomach." His sister-in-law Catherine Trent appeared to be the only person to show him a kindness for which he did not have to pay. She preserved ten pounds of green grape jelly for her dead sister's husband. He did not live to eat it.[3]

The deal that Newman struck with his two Trent nephews John and Stephen on 2 January 1899 was ruled illegal by the Virginia Superior Court following his death, and Belmont was no longer in the hands of a family native to Buckingham County.[4] Two of Newman's West Virginia relatives, his sister Bettie Noland and niece Anne Moore Shorts, challenged his will and won, gaining title to his entire estate, including the property Pattie Newman had transferred to his name.

Wade, Woodson, and Morris family members in 1913. Van Woodson is second from left on back row; his wife, Mary, is second from left on second row holding baby Wiley; their two other children, William Howard and Ethel, are second and third on the front row. Lewis Morris, the first family member to buy land, stands in the middle of the group, the fifth person from the left on the second row.

The Pages and Trents never forgave those outsiders for taking what had been their family's for more than two hundred years, and they never forgave Newman for allowing it to happen, even though he was dead when it did.

Page's descendants stayed on, living in the Union Hill, Carys-wood, and Bell Branch Plantation houses. They employed the descendants of the enslaved people their ancestors had held.

Ten years into the twentieth century, a descendant of Caryswood and Belmont Plantation slaves, a Wade-Morris-Peaks-Woodson-child, was born into the sum total of it all.[5] Her life story illustrates the last-

Ethel Woodson, 1929

ing impact of patronage on a community of material-poor freedmen, the ramifications of land acquisition in the New South, and the kinship networks evidenced through work relationships. The buying habits established generations before her birth and the family lore created before and during her lifetime were as familiar to her as the palms of her hands. Her life story brings all aspects of this community's eighteenth- and nineteenth-century experiences together, day in and day out in the twentieth century.

If the name Booker T. Washington, or the events of the Niagara Movement or World War I made an impact and difference in this rural woman's life, she never mentioned it or them. The events and people of the wider world, black and white, did not fill the life, memories, or consciousness of Ethel Beulah Woodson Bolden. Her mind, memory, and life focused on two worlds–this side, filled with toil and trouble–and the one on the other side, her Father's home where "sabbath has no end." Because Ethel Bolden stayed on the course bordered by these two worlds and never strayed off it to influence the world or let it influence her, she, like many Americans, lived through the early, mid-, and late twentieth century but was not a part of it.

Everyone who remembers the day the midwife drove her wagon over the dirt road to the cabin that Van and Mary Woodson stayed in, beside the big tree at the Union Hill plantation, is dead. It is unknown if the road was slick with rain or sleet or if the midwife had to bundle herself against the cold or wipe away sweat as she made her way to the place where she would help a twenty-two-year-old woman bring her second child in two years into the world. Anyone who would have recalled which of the two area midwives Van Woodson sent for to tend his wife is buried in one of the Piedmont, Virginia, black church graveyards.[6] It could have been Aunt Lucy Harris or Mrs. Branch, but there is no one to say which. No matter what the details of the day, the birth resulted in the first day of life for a healthy girl child, one of the second generation born free but still living on one of the plantations where their ancestors had been held and where they still worked.

Like her brother William Howard, Ethel would have an appearance which hinted at the coming together of several groups of Ameri-

cans. She would not look like her mother or father, but a sure com-
bination of them both. From her dark-skinned, thick-haired mother
she drew a small frame that never held fat but never could be called
thin. Her father was a tall, lean, light-skinned man with gray eyes,
sandy hair, and the sure walk of the Native Americans his people
claimed to have partly been born from. While Van never spoke of the
European Americans who contributed the hue of his eyes and hair,
they were as surely a part of his ancestry as the African Americans
and Native Americans of which he was so proud. Ethel would be one
of the eleven mulatto children born to this couple over a twenty-one-
year period.[7]

Ethel's first memory was sitting in her mother's kitchen on one of
her father's knees with him feeding her milk from a spoon. Her father
could have done this many times during the first years of her life. The
day that stayed in her memory could have been the day of her
brother Wiley's birth, two years after her own.

Perhaps Van quieted his toddler as his wife brought the second of
his seven sons into the world. This memory of her father spoon-
feeding her this way, joined with others, most unspoken, led Ethel
to admit that she liked her father more than she liked her mother
even though he "had a lot of devil in him before he got saved." It could
have been a "little bit of that devil in him" that attracted him to Lizzie
Wade, her mother's paternal aunt and edged him into fathering her
first child, Lillian, during the early years of his marriage to his wife.
Maybe being "saved" kept him from fathering others outside of his
home with Mary.[8]

Ethel's second memory had to do with life and death. In it, she
recalled the day her great-grandfather, Jerry Wade, got the dyin' grace
and went on over to the other side. This event appears to plant and
then anchor her faith in a God who could work miracles for people
like herself. Ethel would live her life trying to get the dyin' grace, and
her brother William Howard would consider it an old man's foolishness and ignore its significance as anything other than a good story.[9]

By the time Ethel was fifteen years old, she had lived on three different white men's places with her family, had witnessed the births of
seven siblings and the death of one, and had entered the work world.
The Woodsons did not stay on at Union Hill longer than five years

after Ethel was born. At Union Hill, the one-and-a-half-story cabin, with two ground-floor rooms and a sleeping loft above, was close to blacks and whites both of her parents were related to or knew. Jerry and Phibbie Wade, Ethel's maternal great-grandparents, had been held at Union Hill before the emancipation and had stayed on there after the Civil War. While the names of the white families who owned Union Hill changed because of marriage unions, the people remained familiar. When Van and Mary moved from Union Hill, they moved to another plantation farm which had originally been part of the Union Hill land tract. They stayed on the Tribles' place, Bell Branch, a shorter time than they had at Union Hill or would at the Keller farm in the following years. Ethel was barely ten years old when she went to work at the Trible plantation house as a cook. She was so young and unskilled that she had to depend on one of the farmhands to help her bake bread for the white family's meals. One of Lizzie Wade's boys had to show how much "soda and salt" to put in the flour to make up the bread. The woman of the house, Gladys Trible, an Irish immigrant, showed Ethel how to cook other foods. Ethel considered the foods that Gladys taught her how to make to be "funny foods" because they were so different from the foods prepared in her mother's kitchen. Gladys Trible was most likely very pleased with Ethel's efforts and progress and tried to help the Woodson family out because by that time "they had so many children." When Trible offered to take Ethel away with her to Massachusetts, Mary Woodson prohibited it saying, "you're too young to go out that far."

A newborn baby joined the Woodson household every two years. All except one had an uneventful entry into the world. When Ethel's sister Teen was born, her birth was especially difficult for both her and her mother. Baby Teen's arm was broken as she made her way into the world. A Dr. Nichols was called upon to examine the infant. He warned that her health was not good and that all care should be taken to keep her well because if she ever became ill, she would surely die. When Ethel was nine years old, her five-year-old sister caught an Asiatic flu and died even though her parents did everything in their power to save her. Ethel and her siblings remember how their mother saved all of Teen's gowns and dresses in the family trunk along with one orange Mary had purchased for her but which the child was too weak to eat. The clothes of course kept over the years, but so did the orange. It did not rot. It simply hardened and darkened in the trunk where Mary Woodson would often go and touch it and the clothes, the last reminders of the child she lost.[10] Ethel came to understand what folks called "a mother's love" from watching her mother when Teen died.

Teen's life and death are sad memories from a household often marred by want but which held much joy. Ethel especially remembers Christmas as being a wonderful time in her childhood home. Each child would get "something big" like a doll and then some smaller things like an orange or some candy. All of the children old enough to walk the distance to their mother's aunt's home were allowed to do so. There they were greeted and fed a holiday meal. The next day, they visited their maternal grandparents Matt and Martha Wade's home where they repeated the ritual. No one left hungry on these days.

Everyone also had enough to eat on the cold winter days when hogs and cows were slaughtered. Ethel recalls that each year her father killed "five hogs and a cow." This meat was kept in a smokehouse or canned for use during the year. Mostly everything else that the family ate came from their mother's garden. The only items the family purchased were "[baking] soda, salt, and a little oil for the lamp." Lamp oil was used only when "company came" in the evenings. When the family was alone after dark, they used "lightwood" to illuminate the front room where they sat around the fire hearth before going to bed. Once tossed into the fireplace, the dried wood would light up the entire room.

For the first eleven years of Ethel's life, she watched lightwood being thrown into the fireplace that her family did not own. When she was twelve, and living at "ol' man Keller's place" right on the Buckingham and Cumberland County line, her father piled his wife, all seven of their children, and all of their furniture into one wagon and boasted, "Y'all goin' home now!" The loaded-down wagon made the short journey over the rocky roads in a short time. The two family dogs, Ring and Sut, gifts to the children from midwife Mrs. Alice Harris, circled the wagon in their own excitement. The dogs would have plenty of snakes, rabbits, and squirrels to kill at the new home.

Van took his family to the twenty-five-acre tract of land which was to be their new home place. After World War I, Virginia tobacco prices had skyrocketed. Van was able to buy the place, former Caryswood Plantation land, with the cash he received from a couple of good tobacco crops he had sharecropped on Washington Keller's property. The house where he took his family only had two rooms at first, but he and his wife added five good-sized rooms onto the structure, another fireplace, a wide front porch, windows with glass panes, and shutters.

At the new family home, Ethel did more than work and watch children come into her household. She also went to church. It was in church that she came alive and became an individual. Her family often traveled to the Zion Baptist Church, which she called "her church," in a wagon with her father at the reins and her mother beside him. Following her parents' and grandparents' example, she was often moved by the Spirit both in and out of church. She remembers hearing her maternal grandfather praying before she reached the house when she was as far away as the spring. In church her mother would sing the same song each time before the service began. Her voice would rise as she rejoiced: "Another day, another day, that the Lord has kept me." The thick heels of the white shoes she wore would click the floor boards of the church as she marched and shouted out her testimony. Van Woodson's tall, lean body jumped up and down, sometimes three feet from the floor, as he boasted, "I got a home, in the rock, don't you see. I got a home in the rock, don't you see. Right in between the earth and the sea, I got a home in the rock don't you see."

After watching them, Ethel yearned and prayed for an opportunity to have such a relationship with God. She gave up the favored activities of her daily life, such as playing checkers, in hope that the Lord would find favor in her and save her from sin. When she was ten years old, she accompanied her brother William Howard and one of her mother's friends, Mrs. Margaret Cane, to an evening service at Zion. Mrs. Cane had invited William Howard (usually called simply Howard) to attend the service because he was nearing the twelve-year-old age when he would be asked to go to the front of the church, sit in the first row of chairs called the mourning bench, and pray to be saved by the Holy Spirit. While Howard remained untouched,

Ethel was moved to tears by the Spirit before she knew it. Tears fell down her cheeks onto her dress. Mrs. Cane asked if she wanted to go up to the front of the church so that everyone could pray for her. She moved from the back of the church to the front where the power fell on her with full force. Ethel remembers singing, crying, and shouting all the way home. No one could quiet her down. She repeated her religion—a verse she would be moved to say whenever she was touched by the Holy Spirit—over and over again as she made her way through the woods. "I thank God. I done died. I thank my God and thank my Jesus, too." Her father met her at the door, alarmed by her cries before she set foot onto the porch. He said, "Bless your heart." Mary Woodson cried tears of joy at the sight of the first one of her children to make an open confession of Christ's power and receiving salvation from the Holy Spirit. Howard had quietly followed his sister's procession home. He did not get the Holy Spirit that night. Ethel asserted, "I don't know what Howard got."

Ethel was not satisfied at just being saved. She wanted the sanctification she had heard talked about as well. Four years after her salvation experience, she attended a tent service conducted by a Philadelphia woman, Ida Robinson. Bishop Robinson had been brought to the community by Ethel's aunt, Annie Wade. When Robinson set up her tent on Buckingham County ground, she was no stranger to shouting or changing black lives. With only a third-grade education—"she had only gotten as far as the third reader"—she had been called to preach, cure afflictions, and save souls. When questioned by authorities, Robinson told lawyers that she had "got [her] education on high and [her] graduation on [her] knees." This still did not explain how she restored sight to the blind, caused the lame to walk, or made twisted limbs straight and grow out before the watchful eyes of her church audience.[11]

Again Ethel sat herself in the back of the congregation. This time, however, there was no need for her to move to the front. The Holy Spirit moved through the tent, touching and setting her on fire. Three grown women tried to hold her down. They could not. She shouted all over the church. She felt like she was in the air. Ida Robinson said, "Y'all let her go, y'all can't do nothing with her."

On this occasion there were only two people sanctified during the tent services, Ethel and her grandmother, Martha Morris Wade. They would found the Bright Morning Star Holiness Church on Wade land.[12] Others would help them build a church building, the third black worship center in the community and the first and only Holiness Church. Van and Mary Woodson would be among them. Van would even go on to become the first deacon at Bright Morning Star. His activities heightened his esteem in his daughter's eyes and made him available to hear her sing her favorite song, "I'm on my way to Canaan Land. I'm on my way to Canaan Land. Thank God. I'm on my way to Canaan Land."

Ethel was not able to attend school on a regular basis. In her own words, she "didn't go too much" but does remember having at least three teachers at the one-room schoolhouse she walked to with brother Howard and then Wiley. Mrs. Lemuel Wade, her daughter Mary Wade, and Miss Lucy Brown would all teach at the Jones School close to the Zion Baptist Church. Ethel had attended enough to learn how to read and write. She had read the Bible all of her life, memorized many verses, preached sermons, and written letters to friends and family whenever the need or desire arose.

At first, work to help support her siblings took her away from the schoolhouse. When her father became ill with cancer in 1930, she was never to return to school again. When Gladys Trible and her family moved away, Ethel joined her mother in the plantation kitchen at Caryswood where she was paid $1.75 a week. She passed the entire sum on to her mother, who used the money to support the seven children still living at home. When Ethel turned fifteen, her mother consented to let her move to the city–Richmond–where no family lived, but where Ethel could get a room with a family friend and find better-paying work. She would work in Richmond, sixty miles from home, for five years, sometimes doing domestic work in private homes and once in a boardinghouse for a short time. Whenever possible, she would return home and spend time at home where her father was dying. She was not there the evening that he died. Her younger sister, Edith, told her about what happened.[13]

Mr. John Swann, "a great friend" of Van's, would come and sit with him each evening toward the end of his life. John Swann would sometimes talk either to God or to his friend at whose bedside he sat.

Sometimes he would sing. At other times he just sat and watched Van slip to the other side. On one fall evening, John noticed that Van had stopped breathing. He lifted his friend up and tried to shake the life back into him. When that did not work, he threw Van down onto the bed, hoping that the action would force the air back into his lungs. All around him, Van's children watched, wishing that these tactics would work. They did not. In the end, the children were angered by John's actions, blaming him for not being able to save their father.

When John Swann walked the length of the front room into the Woodson dining room, he was met there by Van's wife and two of Van's sisters, Martha and Willie Anna. The words that he mumbled, Mary Woodson had heard before. They were like the ones that Van had spoken when he returned from seeing Jerry Wade years before on his death day. Swann said, "Van is gone. . . ."

Van and Mary Woodson had allowed their three oldest children to leave home and work in the city to earn money to support the family. The two sons had gone to Baltimore to work at the Bethlehem Steel Mills which, even during the Depression, was hiring and paying well. Ethel of course was closer to home in Richmond doing domestic work. All three of the oldest children were called home.[14]

The 1932 funeral was a sad one. Wiley fainted at his father's grave site. Others wept. Mary Woodson determined that she would raise the nine children still at home and hold onto the family homestead.[15]

Ethel's sister Edith asserts that things would have been different in Ethel's life if their father had lived. Ethel certainly would not have married the man that she did. Even though Mary tried to persuade her daughter not to marry Alexander "Top" Bolden, Ethel planned to do just that. Mary did not want her daughter to marry Top because he was older than her daughter by twelve years and had been married before to a woman who had died. It seems that Top's first wife Poca had died while giving birth to their second son, John Eddy. Left alone for several days, Poca's body had started to smell before anyone even knew she was dead. Where had Top gone off to—knowing, knowing that his young wife was almost ready to deliver his second child? For Mary Woodson, who had always been tended by midwives at the births of her children, Top's actions were inexcusable and unforgivable.

Stricken by grief and maybe shamed by what happened to his wife, Top left the area, went to New York where he worked for several years. When he was ready to marry again, he, like most of the other men from his community, came back to find himself a wife. He met Ethel at the only place she ever went while she was home from her Richmond work. He met her at church. Ethel does not recall their courtship fondly. She asserts that she does not remember "all that foolishness" that Top did while he courted her. Perhaps she is embarrassed at the course their early love took as she speaks about it fifty-seven years later.

It was not as if Ethel did not have other choices for a husband. A Richmond preacher, William Houston, with "four churches" had also wanted to marry her (Houston was younger than Top), but Top "just kept after her" and she decided to become his wife. When Mary Woodson expressed her displeasure at the marriage prospect, Ethel went into her room, shut the door, and refused to come out. There was "much carrying on." Ethel's oldest brother still at home, Robert, known for his quick temper and sure trigger finger, offered to shoot Top on sight if his mother so wished. She did not. Mary Woodson finally agreed to the wedding and Ethel came out of her room.

After Ethel and Top were married in Richmond, they came back to Buckingham County. Their first home was a cabin on the same farm where he had lived with his first wife and where she had died. Taking no chances that the birth of her first child would not go well, Ethel had Mrs. Mary Thubbs, a midwife who Ethel says was "practically a doctor," called in to take care of her. Ethel says that she "can't forget" what her first birthing experience was like. She assesses simply that "it was hard." Mary Woodson was not there for the birth, but came to see about her daughter and her first grandchild, a boy, William, shortly after he was born. Even though Ethel declares that she "never did want any children," she and Top had two boys, William (named after Ethel's oldest brother), Melvin, and three girls named Alsenda (called Sister by everyone), Roxie, and Mary (named after Ethel's mother but called Geraldine).

It is unclear where Top got the money to buy the family farm. He could have saved it while working in New York. It is most likely, however, that he earned the funds in the early 1940s when he left the area for the second time, leaving his wife and children behind, to work at the Bethlehem Steel Mills in Baltimore. Each Sunday of the two years he spent in Baltimore, Top would put on his Sunday clothes and ride the streetcar to Ethel's sister's house in East Baltimore where he would have dinner with this family from home. At the end of the two-year period, Top returned to Buckingham County, moved his family off the Carruthers land and onto a thirty-acre tract of land for which he paid cash. The house wasn't much to look at, but it sat "right close" to the road and had a spring with good clear water within walking distance.

Like her mother, Ethel Bolden had to work outside of her home to help provide for her family. She did what her mother and her mother's mother had done—she cooked in the Caryswood Plantation kitchen and prayed to the Lord to make her way easier in this world, keep her children safe, and save them all from sin. Ethel remembers that she "worked hard, real hard" trying to raise her children. She tells the two stories that most challenged her over and over again. When trouble came, it came in pairs.

Ethel and Top's two oldest children followed the career examples of their parents. When William was old enough, he went to Baltimore and with the assistance of his mother's brothers, found work at Bethlehem Steel. Their oldest daughter decided to seek work, not in Richmond or Baltimore, but in Philadelphia where she had heard that there were numerous jobs paying good money. Like her mother had done twenty years before, "Sister" rented a room at first and then moved into a flat with a young woman she met from home. Sister did not keep her mother's religious ways, however, and was soon on her way home, unmarried and pregnant with her parent's first grandchild. On the long bus ride home, she wove together a story sure to gain her mother's sympathy and which would relieve herself of all fault and responsibility in her untimely pregnancy.[16] Sister told her parents and everyone who would listen that she had been knocked on the head, rendered unconscious and "bothered." She, like the Virgin Mary, did not remember the carnal act.

Ethel came to her daughter's rescue. She defended Sister against all doubters and decided that she would keep the baby and raise it herself until he was twelve years old and could go out into the world with his mother who returned to her work and life in the city. Grandson Ricky became Ethel and Top's pride and joy. After his birth, the circumstances of his conception were never discussed. Ethel had, by following a Biblical example she knew well, weathered one storm. There was another to come.

Every day of winter 1960, Ethel had warned Top that the chimney was going to catch fire. It was a lean-to chimney and it hadn't been cleaned in too long a time. The house was always filling with smoke. She had pointed this out to him and mentioned it to him more times than she could remember. Her daughter Roxie was the first one to wake up the morning their house caught on fire. Each of the children had been able to stumble down the steps from their sleeping loft out the front door to safety and fresh air except one, her younger son, Melvin. She and Top could hear him calling from the top of the stairs on the other side of the fire. The thick smoke kept him from their view.

Everyone tried to keep Ethel from going after Melvin, but she knew that she had to go save her child. She ran into the house, asked God and his son Jesus to make a way for her to get to him, or at least to just let her see him, and They did. As soon as she uttered her prayer, a piece of the wall caved in, "no bigger than the palm of your hand," letting in the light and fresh air–just enough to allow her to see her son's heel and catch hold of it, pulling him down the stairs to safety.

They helped her prop him up next to the tree in the front yard. Everyone thought that he was dead, but she knew better. She knew what her Lord could do. She prayed and her son coughed and liquid came out of his nose and mouth and he lived. The house burnt down, but her son lived.[17]

Friends and neighbors rallied to support the family. Ethel and Top's children and grandson went to stay with Ethel's mother who lived a short distance away. Top rebuilt the house, this time with electricity, but still did not add indoor plumbing. They still had to use the old outhouse in back and tote water from the well in the front-side yard.

With her children grown, Ethel became more active in the church. She continued to be a missionary in the community, "going from house to house just like Jesus did." She once stated that she really liked to work with souls that were difficult to save. When the head authorities in her denomination tried to make her an evangelist, she turned down the offer, saying that she wished to "continue on only having to answer to God."

Ethel has believed for a long time that God speaks directly to her. She feels that she is especially good at forecasting people's deaths and other life-changing events like marriages and separations. She also believes that God tells her directly if people are good or bad. Once in church she was sitting next to the daughter of the church pianist. As the man was playing away, looking like a picture of health, Ethel says that the Lord spoke to her and said, "He's gonna die." Without thinking, she repeated the message that she had heard aloud. The man's daughter heard her utterance and naturally became very alarmed. "You said that my father is going to die," the young woman said. Ethel would not deny the message she had been given. The man died two weeks later.

God also spoke to her another time about a church member's impending death. On this occasion, the Lord said, "Go tell Elder Jones that Bishop Jones [her husband] is gonna die." Ethel did not repeat that message, not even to herself. Bishop Jones, the head minister at their church, died later on that day.

Three different times when Ethel was very sick, she was visited by ghosts. Each time she thought that she was at death's door; the appearances of the ghosts seemed to push her back from it. The first ghost she saw was the one of her youngest brother, Walker, who died in 1971, right after Thanksgiving. She said that she was alone in the house and heard her dead brother enter by the front door. He came into her bedroom and pulled up a chair close to her bedside and smiled. He was dressed in a "long white robe, trimmed in black just like the kind Elder McKenzie [her former pastor] wears," and he didn't say a word. He just smiled and walked away. On another occasion, she was very sick and was resting on the sofa in her front room. Her father came in that time and stood in front of her and smiled. She remembers this day because two of her cousins had come to see about her earlier that day also. When her mother visited her from the other side, she did more than just smile at her and leave. Her mother reached out and touched her forehead. Her dead mother's touch made her feel so much better she was able to get up and start working once again around the house. Ethel laughs when she relates these stories, recognizing that some may not believe them even though she knows that they are true.

The next time trouble came in pairs, it took both her husband and her oldest daughter. Their passing within months of each other in 1979 is still too painful for her to talk about. The only other topic Ethel Woodson Bolden refused to discuss was slavery. She said that the "old people didn't talk much about it because they came out of slavery and dropped it." There was no need to discuss the pain.

The only other trouble Ethel faced was so strong, it had no need to come in pairs, as it almost singly took her life. She paid no attention to the small spot on the front of her leg. She just kept on doing her work and God's. After a few weeks, the pain got her attention and she started to pray about it. The pain did not go away and the spot got bigger and darker. The doctors tried to treat it as best they could. She continued to pray and to ask others to do the same. The doctors said that if the place did not heal, they would have to operate on it. Her diabetes was making it worse, would not let it heal. They would have to cut it off before it was too late. Ethel told everyone that the doctors did not know that her God, her Savior, was never too late. He was always on time.

Her daughters put her in the hospital. The doctors scheduled her for surgery, but she would not sign. She didn't want to lose her leg. She wanted to get into heaven whole. They scheduled the operation again. She didn't mind because she knew that Jesus would visit her and either cure that leg or take her on back home with him. He did neither.

Her family and friends talked to her and prayed for and with her. She finally agreed to have her leg taken off. She had read in the Bible that if your eye bothers you, cast it out, and she would cast out this leg. She did and she lived. She even got a new leg and learned to walk and shout on it. Not that she has much inclination to walk around too much these days. Some days she "doesn't feel no ways tired." Other days she just sits at her daughter's window and prays and watches the cars go by. She gets to church whenever she can and walks off the spirit if she can't shout it out like she used to. When asked what she wants people to know about her and her life, she responds that "sometimes you get some hard knocks, but you got to live it right. Got to live it right."[18]

Coda

In Birmingham, Alabama, at the National Civil Rights Museum, there is a gallery with replicas of 1960s doorways and windows. Each window and doorway is open just enough to allow the museum visitor to hear the voices of men and women, some black and some white, speak their minds. The things being said behind the doors and on the other sides of the open windows offer private reasons behind public happenings, responses to what has taken place, and foreshadowings of things to come. Stops along this museum corridor are based upon sources that did not come into being to fill books or newspapers, but sources that came into being in spite of themselves to make sense of everyday worlds. These are the best types of sources.

This book taps the same sort of sources, listening in on the internal lives of white folks and black folks as they tried to make ends meet and keep their families together following the Civil War. This was a difficult task for all, challenging those on both sides of the color line. And the way people coped with meeting that challenge has had lasting effects reaching through generations, down to the present.

Edward Page and James Newman, like landowners all over the South, studied how to get and keep good help. Some tactics worked while others did not, creating a turmoil felt by all. People's actions in the Piedmont fields and plantation yards were often determined not only by race but by how they viewed themselves.

African Americans in this community appear to have made property ownership a goal for reasons beyond personal gain, holding the land in trust for others like themselves who needed safe shelters.

The generation born before emancipation worked to feed and to cover their own backs and the backs of their family members. Some of them lived to see their children and their children's children have something more. Material goods offered a way for blacks, like other Americans, to measure success.

Whites and African Americans alike created stories to reason out their lives, stories based on events that took place in their lifetimes and passed them on to their descendants as teachings. While whites were often a part of the stories told by blacks in this community, those stories were not meant to be shared with whites or to entertain those outside of the race. The language and the story lines appear to step away from understandings outside of the group for which they are intended, as a way to keep foreigners out, and the tales safe inside the community.

When I was growing up, my father whistled only in August, because it was only in August that he would open the doors of his car in the middle of the night, letting my mother and all of us children pile in as we headed off "down the country to home," the places discussed in this book. His brisk whistle was matched only by his quickened pace and a smile which seemed to come easier as he prepared to return to the family and friends he had left behind decades before. He drove through the night so as not to have the 1940s and 1950s segregation demons foil a pleasant journey. When he reached home, a cousin often greeted him with a hearty embrace and "I heard you when your tires hit the James River Bridge! I knew that you were here, even before you got here."

The happiness that bred his whistle and quickened his pace as he traveled back home was the result of freedom and family claimed following the Civil War by his formerly enslaved ancestors, who shaped a new reality together with those who had held them in bondage. And while I cannot whistle, both my pace and heart quicken as I find my way back to this place, time and time again, to grab hold of what was there, the good and the not-so-good. I do this, for the same reasons my father did: because it is where "a way was made out of no way" long before I was even thought of, before I was even a gleam in someone's eye.

Appendix

The Cary-Page Family

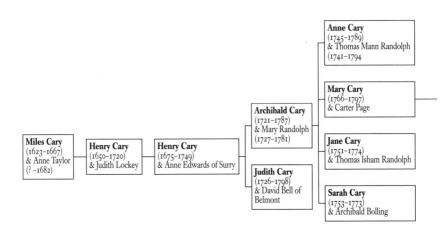

Miles Cary
(1623–1667)
& Anne Taylor
(? –1682)

Henry Cary
(1650–1720)
& Judith Lockey

Henry Cary
(1675–1749)
& Anne Edwards of Surry

Archibald Cary
(1721–1787)
& Mary Randolph
(1727–1781)

Judith Cary
(1726–1798)
& David Bell of Belmont

Anne Cary
(1745–1789)
& Thomas Mann Randolph
(1741–1794

Mary Cary
(1766–1797)
& Carter Page

Jane Cary
(1751–1774)
& Thomas Isham Randolph

Sarah Cary
(1753–1773)
& Archibald Bolling

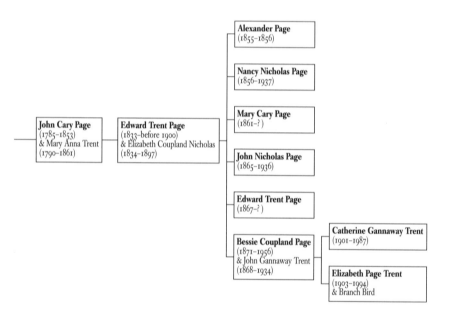

Alexander Page
(1855–1856)

Nancy Nicholas Page
(1856–1937)

Mary Cary Page
(1861–?)

John Cary Page
(1785–1853)
& Mary Anna Trent
(1790–1861)

Edward Trent Page
(1833–before 1900)
& Elizabeth Coupland Nicholas
(1834–1897)

John Nicholas Page
(1865–1936)

Edward Trent Page
(1867–?)

Bessie Coupland Page
(1871–1956)
& John Gannaway Trent
(1868–1934)

Catherine Gannaway Trent
(1901–1987)

Elizabeth Page Trent
(1903–1994)
& Branch Bird

The Gannaway Family

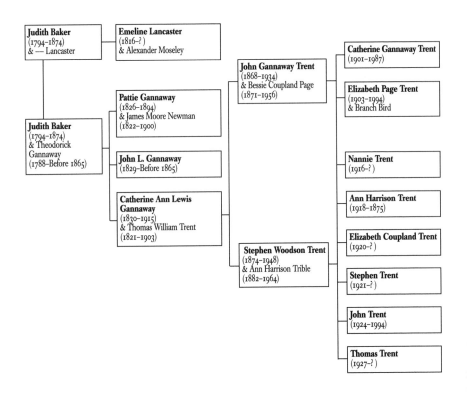

Judith Baker
(1794–1874)
& — Lancaster

Emeline Lancaster
(1816–?)
& Alexander Moseley

Judith Baker
(1794–1874)
& Theodorick
Gannaway
(1788–Before 1865)

Pattie Gannaway
(1826–1894)
& James Moore Newman
(1822–1900)

John L. Gannaway
(1829–Before 1865)

**Catherine Ann Lewis
Gannaway**
(1830–1915)
& Thomas William Trent
(1821–1903)

John Gannaway Trent
(1868–1934)
& Bessie Coupland Page
(1871–1956)

Stephen Woodson Trent
(1874–1948)
& Ann Harrison Trible
(1882–1964)

Catherine Gannaway Trent
(1901–1987)

Elizabeth Page Trent
(1903–1994)
& Branch Bird

Nannie Trent
(1916–?)

Ann Harrison Trent
(1918–1875)

Elizabeth Coupland Trent
(1920–?)

Stephen Trent
(1921–?)

John Trent
(1924–1994)

Thomas Trent
(1927–?)

The Woodson Family

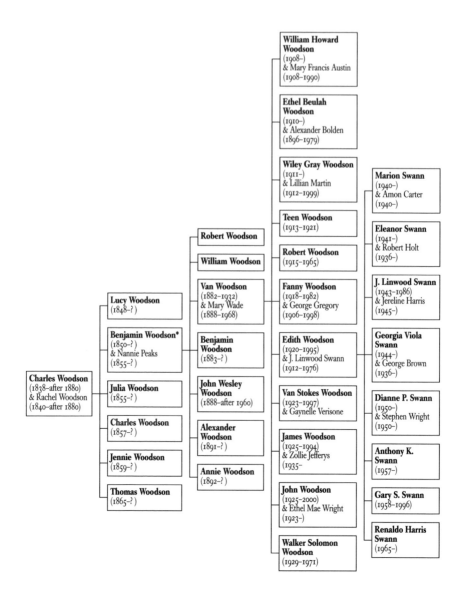

Charles Woodson
(1838–after 1880)
& Rachel Woodson
(1840–after 1880)

Lucy Woodson
(1848–?)

Benjamin Woodson*
(1850–?)
& Nannie Peaks
(1855–?)

Julia Woodson
(1855–?)

Charles Woodson
(1857–?)

Jennie Woodson
(1859–?)

Thomas Woodson
(1865–?)

Robert Woodson

William Woodson

Van Woodson
(1882–1932)
& Mary Wade
(1888–1968)

Benjamin Woodson
(1883–?)

John Wesley Woodson
(1888–after 1960)

Alexander Woodson
(1891–?)

Annie Woodson
(1892–?)

William Howard Woodson
(1908–)
& Mary Francis Austin
(1908–1990)

Ethel Beulah Woodson
(1910–)
& Alexander Bolden
(1896–1979)

Wiley Gray Woodson
(1911–)
& Lillian Martin
(1912–1999)

Teen Woodson
(1913–1921)

Robert Woodson
(1915–1965)

Fanny Woodson
(1918–1982)
& George Gregory
(1906–1998)

Edith Woodson
(1920–1995)
& J. Linwood Swann
(1912–1976)

Van Stokes Woodson
(1923–1997)
& Gaynelle Verisone

James Woodson
(1925–1994)
& Zollie Jefferys
(1935–

John Woodson
(1925–2000)
& Ethel Mae Wright
(1923–)

Walker Solomon Woodson
(1929–1971)

Marion Swann
(1940–)
& Amon Carter
(1940–)

Eleanor Swann
(1941–)
& Robert Holt
(1936–)

J. Linwood Swann
(1943–1986)
& Jereline Harris
(1945–)

Georgia Viola Swann
(1944–)
& George Brown
(1936–)

Dianne P. Swann
(1950–)
& Stephen Wright
(1950–)

Anthony K. Swann
(1957–)

Gary S. Swann
(1958–1996)

Renaldo Harris Swann
(1965–)

The Wade Family

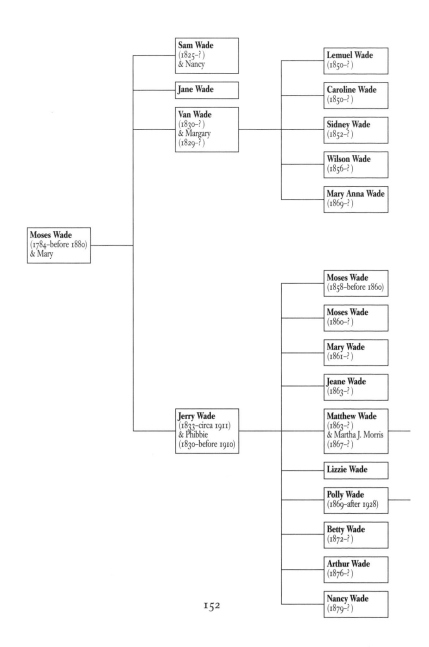

- **Willie Wade**

- **Randy Wade**

- **William Wade**

- **Mary Wade**
  (1888–1968)
  & Van Woodson
  (1882–1932)

- **John Wade**
  & Louise Tyree
  (1903–1992)

- **Vera Wade**
  & Alexander Tyree

- **Annie Wade**

- **Bessie Wade**

- **Maggie Wade**
  & Cary Booker

- **Beverly Lewis Wade**
  & Etta Ford

- **Sarah Bea Wade**
  (1907–1998)
  & Nathaniel Hudson

- **Letcher Bolden Wade**
  (1910–1998)
  & John Corbin

- **Lawrence Wade**
  (1902–?)

- **Nannie Wade**
  (1904–?)

- **Wilson Wade**
  (1906–?)

- **William Howard Woodson**
  (1908–)
  & Mary Francis Austin
  (1908–1990)

- **Ethel Beulah Woodson**
  (1910–)
  & Alexander Bolden
  (1896–1979)

- **Wiley Gray Woodson**
  (1911–)
  & Lillian Martin
  (1912–1999)

- **Teen Woodson**
  (1913–1921)

- **Robert Woodson**
  (1915–1965)

- **Fanny Woodson**
  (1918–1982)
  & George Gregory
  (1906–1998)

- **Edith Woodson**
  (1920–1995)
  & J. Linwood Swann
  (1912–1976)

- **Van Stokes Woodson**
  (1923–1997)
  & Gaynelle Verisone

- **James Woodson**
  (1925–1994)
  & Zollie Jefferys
  (1935–

- **John Woodson**
  (1925–2000)
  & Ethel Mae Wright
  (1923–)

- **Walker Solomon Woodson**
  (1929–1971)

- **William Wade**
  (1920–1929)

- **Senada Pearl Wade**
  (1926–1999)

- **Marion Swann**
  (1940–)
  & Amon Carter
  (1940–)

- **Eleanor Swann**
  (1941–)
  & Robert Holt
  (1936–)

- **J. Linwood Swann**
  (1943–1986)
  & Jereline Harris
  (1945–)

- **Georgia Viola Swann**
  (1944–)
  & George Brown
  (1936–)

- **Dianne P. Swann**
  (1950–)
  & Stephen Wright
  (1950–)

- **Anthony K. Swann**
  (1957–)

- **Gary S. Swann**
  (1958–1996)

- **Renaldo Harris Swann**
  (1965–)

The Swann Family

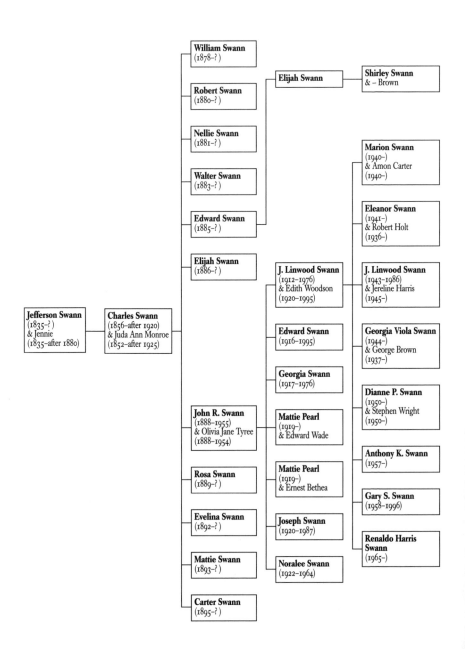

The Morris Family

Alexander Morris
(1836–?)
& Charlotte Trent
(1845–?)

Wilson Morris
(1861–?)

Willie Morris
(1863–?)

Lawrence Morris
(1865–?)

Martha J. Morris
(1867–?)
& Matthew Wade
(1863–?)

Laverne Morris
(1868–?)

Alexander Morris
(1869–?)

Laxamer Morris
(1870–?)

Mary Morris
(1872–?)

Sarah Morris
(1873–?)

Fannie Morris
(1875–?)

Annie Morris

Lewis Morris
(1884–?)

Willie Wade

Randy Wade

William Wade

Mary Wade
(1888–1968)
& Van Woodson
(1882–1932)

John Wade
& Louise Tyree
(1903–1992)

Vera Wade
& Alexander Tyree

Annie Wade

Bessie Wade

Maggie Wade
& Cary Booker

**Beverly Lewis
Wade**
& Etta Ford

Sarah Bea Wade
(1907–1998)
& Nathaniel Hudson

**Letcher Bolden
Wade**
(1910–1998)
& John Corbin

**William Howard
Woodson**
(1908–)
& Mary Francis Austin
(1908–1990)

Ethel Beulah Woodson
(1910–)
& Alexander Bolden
(1896–1979)

Wiley Gray Woodson
(1911–)
& Lillian Martin
(1912–1999)

Teen Woodson
(1913–1921)

Robert Woodson
(1915–1965)

Fanny Woodson
(1918–1982)
& George Gregory
(1906–1998)

Edith Woodson
(1920–1995)
& J. Linwood Swann
(1912–1976)

Van Stokes Woodson
(1923–1997)
& Gaynelle Verisone

James Woodson
(1925–1994)
& Zollie Jefferys
(1935–)

John Woodson
(1925–2000)
& Ethel Mae Wright
(1923–)

**Walker Solomon
Woodson**
(1929–1971)

William Wade
(1920–1929)

Senada Pearl Wade
(1926–1999)

Marion Swann
(1940–)
& Amon Carter
(1940–)

Eleanor Swann
(1941–)
& Robert Holt
(1936–)

**J. Linwood
Swann**
(1943–1986)
& Jereline Harris
(1945–)

**Georgia Viola
Swann**
(1944–)
& George Brown
(1936–)

Dianne P. Swann
(1950–)
& Stephen Wright
(1950–)

**Anthony K.
Swann**
(1957–)

Gary S. Swann
(1958–1996)

**Renaldo Harris
Swann**
(1965–)

The Trent Family

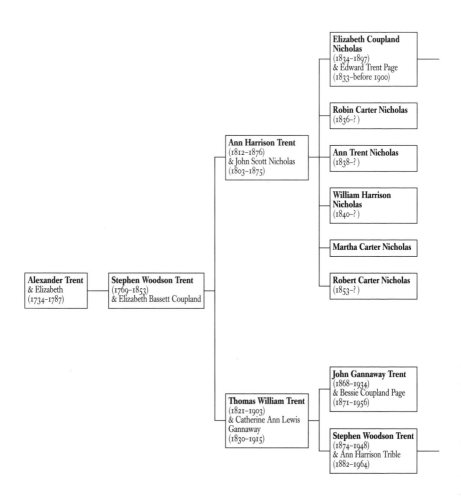

Elizabeth Coupland Nicholas
(1834–1897)
& Edward Trent Page
(1833–before 1900)

Robin Carter Nicholas
(1836–?)

Ann Trent Nicholas
(1838–?)

William Harrison Nicholas
(1840–?)

Martha Carter Nicholas

Robert Carter Nicholas
(1853–?)

Ann Harrison Trent
(1812–1876)
& John Scott Nicholas
(1803–1875)

Alexander Trent
& Elizabeth
(1734–1787)

Stephen Woodson Trent
(1769–1853)
& Elizabeth Bassett Coupland

John Gannaway Trent
(1868–1934)
& Bessie Coupland Page
(1871–1956)

Stephen Woodson Trent
(1874–1948)
& Ann Harrison Trible
(1882–1964)

Thomas William Trent
(1821–1903)
& Catherine Ann Lewis Gannaway
(1830–1915)

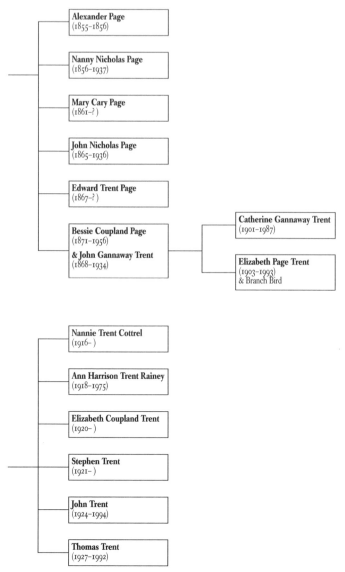

Alexander Page
(1855–1856)

Nanny Nicholas Page
(1856–1937)

Mary Cary Page
(1861–?)

John Nicholas Page
(1865–1936)

Edward Trent Page
(1867–?)

Bessie Coupland Page
(1871–1956)
& John Gannaway Trent
(1868–1934)

Catherine Gannaway Trent
(1901–1987)

Elizabeth Page Trent
(1903–1993)
& Branch Bird

Nannie Trent Cottrel
(1916–)

Ann Harrison Trent Rainey
(1918–1975)

Elizabeth Coupland Trent
(1920–)

Stephen Trent
(1921–)

John Trent
(1924–1994)

Thomas Trent
(1927–1992)

The Tyree Family

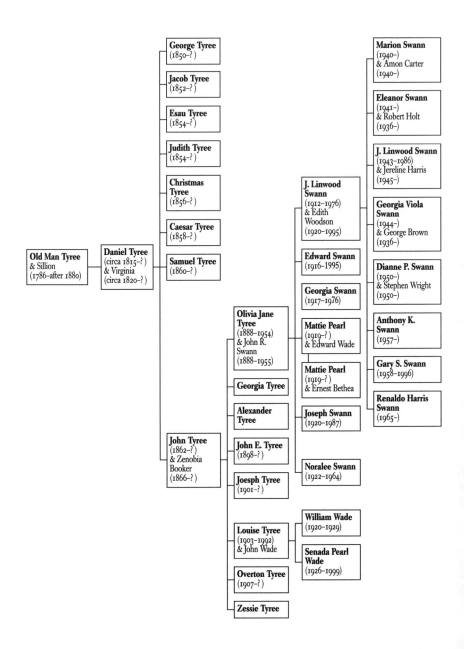

Old Man Tyree
& Sillion
(1786–after 1880)

Daniel Tyree
(circa 1815–?)
& Virginia
(circa 1820–?)

George Tyree
(1850–?)

Jacob Tyree
(1852–?)

Esau Tyree
(1854–?)

Judith Tyree
(1854–?)

Christmas Tyree
(1856–?)

Caesar Tyree
(1858–?)

Samuel Tyree
(1860–?)

John Tyree
(1862–?)
& Zenobia Booker
(1866–?)

Olivia Jane Tyree
(1888–1954)
& John R. Swann
(1888–1955)

Georgia Tyree

Alexander Tyree

John E. Tyree
(1898–?)

Joesph Tyree
(1901–?)

Louise Tyree
(1903–1992)
& John Wade

Overton Tyree
(1907–?)

Zessie Tyree

J. Linwood Swann
(1912–1976)
& Edith Woodson
(1920–1995)

Edward Swann
(1916–1995)

Georgia Swann
(1917–1976)

Mattie Pearl
(1919–?)
& Edward Wade

Mattie Pearl
(1919–?)
& Ernest Bethea

Joseph Swann
(1920–1987)

Noralee Swann
(1922–1964)

William Wade
(1920–1929)

Senada Pearl Wade
(1926–1999)

Marion Swann
(1940–)
& Amon Carter
(1940–)

Eleanor Swann
(1941–)
& Robert Holt
(1936–)

J. Linwood Swann
(1943–1986)
& Jereline Harris
(1945–)

Georgia Viola Swann
(1944–)
& George Brown
(1936–)

Dianne P. Swann
(1950–)
& Stephen Wright
(1950–)

Anthony K. Swann
(1957–)

Gary S. Swann
(1958–1996)

Renaldo Harris Swann
(1965–)

Notes

1. Fairfax Harrison, *The Virginia Carys,* 91–104.

2. Cary, Trent, and Page family trees are given in the Appendix.

3. At the time of this entry, James Moore Newman (1822–1900) was a forty-five-year-old merchant in Evergreen, Virginia. The money in his possession was the proceeds from the sale of his store, 89 acres of land, home, and outhouses. The reasons behind Newman's decision to move out of this area are unclear. After the sale of his store and residence, Newman returned to his hometown, Levels, West Virginia. A little over a year later he returned to the Virginia Piedmont where he married Pattie Gannaway, heir to a 265-acre plantation, Belmont. James Newman, Evergreen Store Ledger, March 1867 entry, 7–8, 15–18 (quote from 18), James Newman Papers, Caryswood Plantation, Buckingham County, Virginia (hereafter referred to as JMNPP). Appomattox Courthouse records.

4. Polly Wade (1868–1928) was the daughter of Phibbie and Jerry Wade, former Union Hill Plantation African American slaves. By the time she was twelve years old, Wade was working outside her family's household as a servant. Both of her parents and two of her eight siblings worked on Newman's Belmont Farm. Wade never married. She did have three children who lived within her parents' household with her until her parents died. She worked all of her life on plantation farms in Buckingham and Cumberland Counties, Virginia, either as a servant or a tobacco stripper. U.S. Federal Census, Ninth, Tenth, Twelfth, and Thirteenth Population Schedules (1870–1910), Buckingham and Cumberland Counties, Virginia. Interviews with William Howard Woodson, 2 August 1993; Ethel Woodson Bolden, 4 July 1992; Wiley Gray Woodson, 25 November 1993; and Edith Woodson Swann, 15 October 1993.

5. For a discussion of the importance of telling a people's story in terms the people themselves would understand, see T. H. Breen and Stephen Innes, *Myne Owne Ground,* 5.

6. The term "community" is used here advisedly because there is so much separation within the study area. For a working definition of the term and a definition of how it is considered in this framework, see Darrett B. Rutman and Anita H. Rutman, *A Place in Time,* 22–31. The Rutmans assert that the term "community" refers to a network existing even in places like this particular study area that can be considered by most observers then and now to be hostile to any indigenous sense of community.

7. In 1880, of the 15,540 people living in the county, 8,773 were black and 6,676 were white. Only 61 persons were born in states other than Virginia. Most

Americans born outside of Virginia came from northern states: 47 from Pennsylvania, 6 from Maryland, and 3 from New York. Foreigners numbered 60, most of them born in England. U.S. Department of the Interior, *Compendium of the Tenth Census.*

8. "Lift Every Voice and Sing," considered by many to be the Negro National Anthem, was written in 1900 by James Weldon Johnson (1871–1938). A writer, civil rights activist, and scholar, Johnson wrote the lyrics, and his brother, J. Rosamond Johnson, set them to music honoring Abraham Lincoln's birth. The song recognized the importance of pressing on in difficult times and under adverse conditions. For more on James Weldon Johnson, see Rachel Kranz's *Biographical Dictionary of Black Americans,* New York, 1992.

9. Jonathan Wiener, "Planter Persistence and Social Change"; C. Vann Woodward, *The Burden of Southern History,* 17; Eric Foner, *Reconstruction,* 128; Jacqueline Jones, *Labor of Love, Labor of Sorrow,* 44–78; Gerald Jaynes, *Old South, New South;* Gavin Wright, *Old South New South,* 12–16; Edward L. Ayers, *The Promise of the New South,* especially 189–213.

10. Hal S. Barron, *Those Who Stayed Behind;* Leon Litwack, *Trouble in Mind;* Jeffrey R. Kerr-Ritchie, *Freedpeople in the Tobacco South.*

11. Eric R. Wolf, *Europe and the People without History.*

12. Darrett B. Rutman and Anita H. Rutman, *A Place in Time.*

13. Caryswood Farm is located in Buckingham County, Virginia. Buckingham County was originally part of Henrico County (1634–1728). Later, it formed part of Goochland County before becoming part of St. Anne's Parish in Albermarle County (1744–1761). Portions of Buckingham County became parts of smaller Cumberland and Appomattox Counties to its east and south. Eugene A. Maloney, *A History of Buckingham County,* 4–5.

14. Historic Buckingham, Inc., *The Geographic Center of Virginia.*

15. Margaret A. Pennington and Loma S. Scott, *The Courthouse Burned,* 130, 161, 165, 166, and 174. H. J. Eckenrode, *The Randolphs: The Story of a Virginia Family,* 40–43.

16. David Bell, for example, was a Buckingham County representative to the House of Burgesses before joining other colonists against England. Another example of this area's leadership in the revolutionary cause is John Fleming from neighboring Cumberland County, who cooperated with Patrick Henry to gain passage of a resolution against the Stamp Act. Major Carter Page had an even higher profile, serving as Lafayette's aide-de-camp. Others such as Archibald Cary had more personal and less virtuous reasons for going against the Crown. Cary borrowed 3,975 pounds from Colony Speaker and Treasurer John Robinson to offset his own personal debts. Robinson illegally loaned the funds to Cary from the colony's tax funds. It was in Cary's best interest to stay as far away from England's control as possible after this act had been committed and he had reached a point where he either determined not to repay the debt or became unable to do so. See Virginius Dabney, *Virginia: The New Dominion,* 113–116; and J. D. Martin, *Today and Yesterday in the Heart of Virginia,* 227–231.

17. Isaac Jefferson's recollections of Archibald Cary are reprinted in James A. Bear, *Jefferson at Monticello.*

18. Harrison, *The Virginia Carys,* 93.

19. See *Virginia Gazette,* 1 August 1766, 15 February 1700, for samples of Buckingham County runaway advertisements.

20. Buckingham Baptist Church Minute Book, 1868, 19 December 1868 entry, unnumbered page, Buckingham Baptist Church archive, Dillwyn, Va.

21. Cumberland County Courthouse Order Book 45, 1851–1857, 24 September 1855, 401, Cumberland Courthouse, Cumberland, Va.

22. Maloney, *A History of Buckingham County,* 61.

23. Edward T. Page, Half-Way Branch Account and Expense Book, August 1862, 1 March 1864, Edward T. Page Papers, Caryswood Plantation, Dillwyn, Va. (hereafter referred to as ETPPP). See James I. Robertson, Jr., *Civil War Virginia: Battleground for a Nation,* and Frank E. Vandiver, *Their Tattered Flags,* for discussions of this area's role in the Civil War; and James H. Brewer, *Confederate Negro* for stories of black involvement in the Confederate war efforts.

24. Pennington and Scott, *The Courthouse Burned,* 130.

25. Maloney, *A History of Buckingham County,* 69.

26. Jeanne Stinson, *A Pictorial History of Dillwyn, Virginia,* 1–12.

27. Maloney, *A History of Buckingham County,* 63–65.

28. Stinson, *Pictorial History,* 8–10.

29. Andrew Buni, *The Negro in Virginia Politics,* 22.

30. James Newman, Farm Book Two, November 1885 diary entries, JMNPP. Buni, *Negro in Virginia Politics,* 2–49.

31. Stinson, *Pictorial History,* 10–24.

1. Patronage

1. Half-Way Branch Account and Expense Book, ETPPP. Elizabeth Page Trent Bird (1903–1993), interview, 29 September 1991.

2. John C. Page was one of the top slaveholders in the county. Only two of his neighbors, Powhatan Jones and Alexander Trent, held more persons than Page in this community. U.S. Bureau of the Census, Federal Census, Eighth Population Schedule, 1860, Buckingham County, Va.

3. Virginius Dabney, *Virginia: The New Dominion;* J. D. Martin, *Today and Yesterday in the Heart of Virginia;* and *Virginia Magazine of Genealogy* 28, no. 2 (May 1990): 87–95.

4. While Page did not keep a running tab of how much of his father's money he actually spent building and furnishing his new home, his father John C. Page was well aware of how much of his money his son used. John Cary wrote in his will that he had given his son $24,000. His expressed intention was for Edward not to have spent more than $20,000 and he wished upon his death that Edward repay his over expenditure back to his father's estate. It is not evident from Edward Page's records that he carried out his father's desire. John C. Page Will, Will

Book 12, 110, Cumberland County Courthouse, Cumberland County, Va. Edward T. Page, Half-Way Branch Account and Expense Book, entries for 1854, ETPPP.

5. Edward Page wrote of the debt of the horses to the Confederate Government. The enslaved Frank who was hired out to the government may have come back to this community after the war but as a free man. Page lists having a blacksmith named Frank after the war but does not list a last name. Edward T. Page, Half-Way Branch Account and Expense Book, Leather Pocket Notebook (both in ETPPP).

6. Newman recorded his parents' birth and death days in a leather pocket notebook listing everything that he owned. He counted their lives down to the day. James Newman, Leather Pocket Notebook One, inside front cover, JMNPP.

7. James Newman Personal Papers Box One, items dated 1866–1869, JMNPP.

8. Randy Kidd and Jeanne Stinson, *Virginia Historic Marriage Register.*

9. U.S. Bureau of the Census, Federal Census, Ninth Population Schedule, 1870, Buckingham County, Va.

10. Stephen Innes, *Labor in a New Land,* 175.

11. Carter G. Woodson, *The Rural Negro,* 46.

12. Ibid., 45.

13. Crandall Shifflett, *Patronage and Poverty in the Tobacco South,* 25.

14. Woodson, *The Rural Negro,* 54.

15. Samuel T. Bitting, *Rural Land Ownership among the Negroes in Virginia.* For Booker T. Washington's public stance on Negro education and on work opportunities for blacks, see his *Up from Slavery,* and Louis R. Harlan's *Booker T. Washington: The Making of a Black Leader, 1856–1901* (New York, 1972) and *Booker T. Washington: The Wizard of Tuskegee, 1901–1915* (New York, 1983).

16. Lewis Morris was one of the most colorful and uncontrollable people in this community. Most informants, black or white, have at least one Lewis Morris story to share. Interestingly enough, while whites considered Lewis Morris wasteful, he was the first person in his family and one of the first in the black community to purchase land. Buckingham County Deed Book 22, 89. Elizabeth Page Trent Bird, interview, 29 September 1991. William Howard Woodson, interview, 13 August 1993. Ethel Woodson Bolden, interview, 15 October 1993. James M. Newman, Farm Book Two (JMNPP).

17. It has been both challenging and rewarding documenting the residential place of African Americans before and immediately following the Civil War. Because the Buckingham Courthouse burned in 1869, no bills of sale filed there are extant. The wills of Edward T. Page's father and grandfather, who both resided in Cumberland County and whose wills were filed in the courthouse there, proved most useful. When Carter Page's slaves were assessed for probate in 1825, only the first name, age, and market value for each was listed. John C. Page's appraisers did not consider individuals for assessment but appraised the value of family groups. Comparing Carter's 1825 will with John's 1853 will shows that both slave populations were counted in similar orders. For example, a Jenny follows a Moses on the Carter Page will and a Moses and a Jenny are assessed together on the John

Page will. In another instance, a Reuben and a Shadrack are separated by one name on the Carter Page will and are assessed together on the Carter Page will around twenty-five years later. The name between Reuben and Shadrack belonged to a female, Harriet, who was willed to one of Carter Page's daughters and lived in her own home. U.S. Bureau of the Census, Federal Census Slave Schedules, Tenth Census 1860, Curdsville District, Buckingham County, Va.; Carter Page Will, Will Book 8, 89, Cumberland County Courthouse, Cumberland, Va.; and John Cary Page Will, Will Book 12, 145, Cumberland Courthouse, Cumberland, Va.

18. John Burdick, "From Virtue to Fitness" (quote on p. 22).

19. Letter to Catherine Gannaway (Trent) from A. C. Page of Goochland, Va., ETPPP. A. C. Page is one of the Archibald Cary Pages who lived at Tuckahoe Plantation in Goochland County, Va.

20. Catherine Trent gave birth to her first child, John Gannaway Trent, on 20 November 1868. John G. Trent would grow up and marry Edward Page's daughter, Bessie, in 1890. Gannaway, Trent, and Page Family Bibles (Trent Family Archive and ETPPP).

21. James M. Newman, Leather Pocket Notebook One, April 1865 entries, JMNPP.

22. U.S. Bureau of the Census, Federal Census, Ninth Non-Population Schedule, 1870, Buckingham County, Va.

23. James M. Newman, Leather Pocket Notebook Two, 3 March 1870, 3, JMNPP.

24. U.S. Bureau of the Census, Federal Census, Ninth Non-Population Schedule, 1870, Buckingham County, Va.

25. U.S. Bureau of the Census, Federal Census, Ninth Agricultural and Production Schedule, 1870, Buckingham County, Va.

26. Shifflett, *Patronage and Poverty*, 24–26.

27. James M. Newman, Farm Book Two, Livestock Insurance account sheet, 37, JMNPP.

28. Edward T. Page, Half-Way Branch Account and Expense Book, ETPPP. James M. Newman, Farm Book One, JMNPP. U.S. Bureau of the Census, Federal Census, Eighth Population Schedule, 1860, Buckingham County, Va.

29. Burdick, "From Virtue to Fitness," 28.

30. Bitting, *Rural Land Ownership*, 70.

31. W. E. B. DuBois, "The Negroes of Farmville," 25–30.

32. Edward T. Page, Half-Way Branch Account and Expense Book, Anthony Cooper account sheets, 22–23 January 1870 entries, 15, ETPPP.

33. Page consistently paid taxes for two of his workers, Morgan and Anderson Ross. Edward T. Page, Half-Way Branch Account and Expense Book, Morgan Ross and Anderson Ross account sheets for 1867, ETPPP.

34. Edward T. Page Personal Papers, Folders One and Two; Leather Pocket Notebook, Gerry Wade, Daniel Brown, and Van Wade entries, ETPPP.

35. Edward T. Page, Leather Pocket Notebook, page headed by date April 12, 1867, ETPPP.

36. Edward T. Page, Leather Pocket Notebook, Daniel Brown, Nelson Peaks, Van Wade, Sam Wade, and Gerry Wade account sheets, ETPPP.

37. ETPPP, Folders One and Two.

38. Edward T. Page, Leather Pocket Notebook, Nelson Peaks account sheet, ETPPP.

39. James M. Newman, Farm Book Two, Davy Harris account sheet, entries 6 November 1886 thru June 1887, 128, JMNPP.

40. ETPPP, Folder One, Exempted Property Form No. 20 dated 14 November 1873. Page lists that he owned, among other things, the following items: wearing apparel, fifteen bushels of corn, one ox cart, one wagon, farming tools, two horses, one mule and one yoke of oxen.

41. James M. Newman, Leather Pocket Notebook Two, 3 November 1869 entry and 27 October 1870, unnumbered pages, JMNPP.

42. James M. Newman, Leather Pocket Notebook Two, 16 and 22, JMNPP.

43. Newman was aware of special auctions and estate sales in Richmond because he read the *Richmond Dispatch*. The auction that he attended in 1878 was off the beaten path in Richmond, more than ten blocks away from the more prominent auction houses that advertised on a regular basis. Newman probably also went to Richmond with some apprehension. The same papers that advertised the sales also carried numerous articles detailing the crime that took place in the city. *Richmond Dispatch,* February and March 1878. Quotes from James M. Newman, Leather Pocket Notebook Three, 23–24, JMNPP.

44. James M. Newman, Farm Book One, Jerry Wade account sheet, 17 February through 17 April 1883, 41, JMNPP.

45. James M. Newman, Farm Book Three, Daniel Brown account sheet, 15 September through 10 November 1890, 7, JMNPP.

46. Edward T. Page, Half-Way Branch Account and Expense Book, account page titled Debts, ETPPP.

47. James M. Newman, Farm Book Two, Stallion and Colt account sheet, 37, JMNPP.

48. Ibid., Blacksmith and James Harris (Carpenter) account sheets, 54 and 41.

49. Ibid., James Harris (Carpenter) account sheet, 41.

50. Ibid., John Trible account sheet, 76.

51. ETPPP, C. H. Harris medical care receipts.

52. James M. Newman, Leather Pocket Notebook Two, inside front cover, JMNPP.

53. Shifflett, *Patronage and Poverty,* 34–37.

54. Woodson, *The Rural Negro,* 47.

2. Work Relationships

1. James Moore Newman was born on 3 October 1822 to John Newman (1754–1826) and Judith Moore Newman (1781–1828), near Levels Township in Hampshire County, Virginia. (Hampshire County became a part of West Virginia

in 1861, refusing with other western Virginian counties to leave the Union.) Judith M. Newman had been married before and had given birth to eight other children before her youngest, James, was born. Newman does not mention that he received an inheritance from either of his parents. He does not write about his early life or education. From diary entries of 1866–1867, written when he visited his hometown following the Civil War and before he married, it appears that the Newmans and Moores lived in a rural community and did quite a bit of hunting and fishing. Newman's first journal was started 29 September 1852 when he was thirty years old and working as a store clerk in the Virginia Piedmont. It is unclear why he came to this area, over 150 miles from his home. One of his brothers, a Rev. William Moore, a Baptist minister in this area, may have encouraged Newman's move. Newman roomed and boarded with him. James M. Newman, Evergreen Store Ledger and Journal, Leather Pocket Notebook One (JMNPP).

2. Newman kept the addresses of several of his siblings written on the inside covers of his leather pocket notebooks. He also kept in touch with them through irregular correspondence. It was in one such letter, William H. Moore to James Newman 12 February 1899 (JMNPP), that he receives word about this particular sister.

3. James M. Newman, Evergreen Store Ledger and Journal, JMNPP.

4. Pattie Gannaway (1826–1894) was forty-two years old when she married James Newman. It was the first marriage for them both. She was the first of three children born to Theodorick and Judith Baker Lancaster Gilliam Gannaway. Both of her parents came from families who had been in the region since before the Revolutionary War. Her older half-sister, Emeline Gilliam, married an attorney, Alexander Moseley, and moved to another part of Buckingham County. Her brother John was killed in the Civil War. His wife lived at the plantation quarter next to Belmont, Cold Comfort. Her sister Catherine married John L. Trent, a relative of the Caryswood and Union Hill families, and moved into the adjacent plantation, Bell Branch. Trent, a Civil War veteran, served as justice of the peace and an election poll judge, as well as treasurer and trustee of Cedar Baptist Church. Pattie Gannaway took care of her father when he became ill in the early 1860s and accompanied him to a mineral springs resort in hopes that the treatments would improve his health. By the time she married Newman (Christmas 1868) her family had done business with Newman for ten years. U.S. Bureau of the Census, Federal Census, Fourth through Ninth Population Schedules, 1820–1870, Buckingham County, Virginia. Trent Family Papers. JMNPP: Evergreen Store Ledger and Journal, Leather Pocket Notebook One, receipts and county voting registration papers.

5. Rosa G. Williams, *Historical Inventory of Buckingham County,* Vol. 1, 108.

6. James M. Newman, Farm Book Two, 2 September 1886, unnumbered page, JMNPP.

7. Ibid., 54.

8. Ibid., 46.

9. Ibid., 25.

10. Ibid., 33–34. This incident took place during March 1887. Newman referred to it on the following days: 2 March, 3 March, 13 March, 18 March.

11. Newman made his first reference to African Americans by skin color in 1869, when he took over Belmont management at his widowed mother-in-law's request. Of the sixteen "hands" whom he employed, Newman listed thirteen of them as "colored" and two as "yellow men"; two did not have any skin color identification next to their names: they were identified by occupation (blacksmith) and status before the war (freed). Newman continued this practice for more than twenty years. It was only during the last years of his life that he omitted the skin color identification labeling. James Newman, Leather Pocket Notebook Three and Farm Books One, Two, and Three, JMNPP.

12. See photograph of a young Matt Wade and his parents, Jerry and Phibbie, in Introduction.

13. James Newman, Farm Book Three, 57, JMNPP.

14. Ibid., 78.

15. Ibid., 88.

16. Ibid., 123.

17. Alexander Morris worked for James Newman, off and on, over a period of twenty years. I have been unable to find out where Morris and his family resided during most of this period. During his tenure at Belmont from 8 January 1887 to 28 July 1890, his household was three-generational: his father-in-law, William Trent (b. 1798, d. unknown), Morris, his wife, and unmarried children. U.S. Bureau of the Census, Federal Census, Tenth Population Schedule, 1880, Buckingham County, Va.

18. James M. Newman, Farm Book Three, 57, JMNPP.

19. Ibid., 102.

20. James M. Newman, Farm Book Two, 68.

21. Ibid., 17 January 1883, 42.

22. The 1870 Federal Census shows the John Gregory family entry listed directly under the entry for the Judith Gannaway, James Newman, and Pattie Newman household. Through oral interviews, I have been able to verify that when families are listed next to each other, they are either neighbors or residing on the same property. The Gregory family is listed as having their own residence, of course, but they could have well lived in one of the five slave quarters that were listed on the 1860 Census as housing the nineteen Belmont slaves. U.S. Bureau of the Census, Federal Census, Eighth and Ninth Population Schedules, 1860 and 1870, Buckingham County, Va.

23. James M. Newman, Farm Book Two, 63 and 64, JMNPP.

24. Ibid., quotes from page 63 with entry dates 23 January 1885 to 21 December 1886.

25. Ibid., 63 and 64 (this and following paragraph).

26. Ibid., 64.

27. U.S. Bureau of the Census, Federal Census, Ninth Population Schedule, 1870, Buckingham County, Va.

28. James M. Newman, Farm Book Three, entry for 22 April 1889, 75, JMNPP.

29. By 1880, George and Amanda Holman had at least three children. U.S. Bureau of the Census, Federal Census, Tenth Population Schedule, 1880, Buckingham County, Va.

30. W. E. B. Du Bois estimated that a family of five could be fed for $3.50 per week during this time period in the rural South. Du Bois, "The Negroes of Farmville, Virginia: A Social Study." The six dollars per month that Holman earned, even when supplemented by the meal and bacon Newman provided as findings, would not have been enough to feed his family. The bacon Newman provided equaled forty-five to sixty slices of meat and the cornmeal could have made only one pan of cornbread per day. These estimates were derived by comparing Southern regional recipes and questioning present-day inhabitants about the dietary habits of their parents and grandparents.

31. James M. Newman, Farm Book Three, entries for 22 April 1889 to 31 May 1889, 75 and 112, JMNPP.

32. Ibid., 112.

33. In 1870, Newman attended an auction at "Valentine's" and purchased many items of used men's clothing. He often did business with a peddler and may have purchased clothing from him also to use as payment for the worker's time. The women's clothes that he paid workers in all came from his wife's closet. He designated them, Pattie's old hats, gloves, and dresses. James M. Newman, Leather Pocket Notebooks Two and Three, Farm Books Two and Three, JMNPP.

34. U.S. Bureau of the Census, Federal Census, Tenth Population Schedule, 1880, Buckingham County, Va.

35. The word "place" was used to stand for a home or a farm. Not having land or access to land through marriage, Holman did not have a "place," but Bryant did.

36. James M. Newman, Farm Book Three, 127, JMNPP.

37. Ibid.

38. That Bryant and not Holman had access to transportation was significant. African Americans were handicapped not only by a lack of land and capital but also because they did not have access to tools. See Crandall Shifflett's *Patronage and Poverty in the Tobacco South,* and Daniel's *Breaking the Land,* for discussions of the importance of having farm tools.

39. James M. Newman, Farm Book Three, 127, JMNPP.

40. Ibid., 127.

41. Ibid., 127.

42. Ibid., 128.

43. Ibid., 127.

44. Ibid., 128.

45. Ibid.

46. It was not usual for African American women to be absent from the fields that their husbands worked. The wives of workers in this study were not charac-

teristic of other African American women living in the New South. For the work habits of African American women, see Jacqueline Jones, *Labor of Love, Labor of Sorrow,* and Herbert Gutman, *The Black Family in Slavery and Freedom.*

47. James M. Newman, Farm Book Three, 36, JMNPP.

48. Shifflett, *Patronage and Poverty,* 35.

49. Cited ibid., 34. The Homestead Exemption Act mandated that all agricultural loans be recorded at county courthouses. Borrowers' liens were thereby noted in the record, so that lenders had a civil record of their investment. The law also granted the borrower the right to set aside $2,000 of his possessions as exempt. The exempted property could not be claimed to satisfy the loan in the event the crop failed. Borrowers often waived this protection of the law and ended up losing everything.

50. James M. Newman, Farm Book Three, 36, JMNPP.

51. Ibid.

52. Ibid., 94.

53. Ibid.

54. Ibid.

55. Ibid.

56. Ibid., 95.

57. This list is a compilation of fabric purchased from 2 February 1888 to 14 November 1890. Ibid., 94–95.

58. Ibid. Harris purchased spools of thread on 2 February 1888, 17 January 1889, and 16 September 1889, for example.

59. Ibid. Harris purchased eight quarts of kerosene in the eleven months between February 1888 and January 1889.

60. Ibid. On an average the African American man contributed ten cents or about one-half a day's pay to church from his Belmont earnings. Ella Harris's tithe was fifty cents for the Association and Church on Holy Days and between ten and twenty-five cents for regular services; that amount represented a higher portion of her income. She only earned about twenty cents a day.

61. It is especially difficult tracing the activities of African American women in the New South. Many times their births and marriages were not recorded, or if they were, they were listed under erroneous surnames. To overcome this problem, a search was conducted of area funeral home programs, looking at the names of the deceased mother. Often the mother of the deceased person was listed by her first, maiden, and married name, in that order. Ella Harris's marriage to Isaiah "Zee" Ayers was found in this way. Children of the deceased person were then contacted and interviewed. The interview information could then be confirmed through other interviews, family papers, Bible entries, and courthouse documents. In this case, one of Ella Harris Ayers's granddaughters, Julia, was interviewed and provided information about her grandmother's early married life that had been passed down to her from her father, Ella's son, Walker. A family Bible in Julia Ayers Anderson's possession confirmed the birth dates and deaths of the Ella Harris Ayers's offspring. Julia Ayers Anderson, interview, 12 July 1993.

62. For a discussion of the characteristics of the work of rural African Americans in the 1880s, see Jones, *Labor of Love, Labor of Sorrow*, 18–19 and 58–60.

63. Ibid., 54.

64. James M. Newman, Farm Book One, 68 (JMNPP).

65. James M. Newman, Farm Book Two, 2–3, JMNPP.

66. Jones, *Labor of Love, Labor of Sorrow*, 57.

67. James M. Newman, Farm Book Two, 60, JMNPP.

68. James M. Newman, Farm Book Three, 11, JMNPP.

3. Land Acquisition

1. By 1874 sixty-year-old John Gregory and his forty-nine-year-old wife considered themselves married for more than twenty-five years. Even though slave unions were not recognized as legal in Virginia and there are no extant church records recognizing their marriage, the Gregorys must have marked the months before the birth of their oldest child as the beginning of their "marriage." In 1870, all eleven of the Gregory children are listed as living at home. The four boys and seven girls ranged in age from twenty-five to five. All of them, owing to the condition of their parents, or more specifically to that of their mother, had been born slaves. U.S. Bureau of the Census, Federal Census, Ninth Population Schedule, 1870, Buckingham County, Va. This first Gregory land purchase is recorded in Deed Book 2, p. 295, Buckingham County Courthouse, Buckingham, Va.

2. Records stating the sale date, size, and cost of the first Winn land purchase are not extant. The John Winn family is not listed on schedules for freed blacks in the 1860 census for this community. Winn most probably worked as a blacksmith on one of the area plantations where he was held. It is also possible that his services were hired out before the war. The descendants of John Winn are the only persons in this community with this surname, suggesting that he was not held by one of the area white families. John Winn is identified in the 1870 census as one of three Curdsville blacksmiths, and the only African American with this trade. Able to own his own business, Winn earned the funds to purchase land faster than his black counterparts who worked as farm laborers. U.S. Bureau of the Census, Federal Census, Ninth Population Schedule, 1870, Buckingham County, Va.; Buckingham County Deed Book 1, unnumbered page.

3. The record telling when Dabney Harris purchased his first parcel of land is not extant. The first courthouse document listing land sales after the 1869 courthouse fire starts in 1870. It shows that Harris purchased the plot which he sold to the Gregorys from Albert Seay, another white man in the community. Neither Harris nor Seay are listed in the 1860 census as owning slaves in the Curdsville District of Buckingham County. U.S. Bureau of the Census, Federal Census, Eighth Population Schedule, 1860, Buckingham County, Va. Buckingham County Deed Book 1, unnumbered page.

4. Buckingham County Deed Book 4, 125.

5. T. H. Breen and Stephen Innes conclude that land ownership opened a

window of opportunity for Tidewater Virginia blacks which was permanently closed by evolving race-based attitudes reflected in the law. Because racial attitudes toward blacks had changed significantly during the colonial and antebellum years, the successes that Anthony Johnson and his family experienced could not have been repeated anywhere in the South following the Civil War. Breen and Innes, *Myne Owne Ground,* quotes taken from 6 and 17.

6. Booker T. Washington to George Washington Cable, 8 October 1889, in *Booker T. Washington Papers,* ed. Louis R. Harlan, Stuart B. Kaufman, and Raymond Smock (7 vols., Urbana. Ill., 1974), cited by Pete Daniel, "The Metamorphism of Slavery, 1865–1900," *Journal of American History* 66 (June 1979): 97.

7. James Russell, "Rural Economic Progress of the Negro in Virginia," *Journal of Negro History* 11 (October 1926): 560.

8. Rhys Isaac, *The Transformation of Virginia,* 31 and 305–306.

9. Herbert Gutman, *The Black Family in Slavery and in Freedom, 1750–1925,* 209 and 331–332.

10. Crandall Shifflett, *Patronage and Poverty in the Tobacco South,* xv and 95.

11. Jacqueline Jones, *Labor of Love, Labor of Sorrow,* 100–102.

12. Loren Schweninger, *Black Property Owners in the South, 1790–1915,* 173.

13. Isaiah Ayers is listed in the 1900 population as being mulatto. U.S. Bureau of the Census, Federal Census, Twelfth Population Schedule, Buckingham County, Va. Julia Ayers Anderson, interview by author, 12 July 1993.

14. James M. Newman, Farm Book Three, 134, JMNPP.

15. Ibid.

16. For the first year that Ella Harris worked for James Newman all of her earnings were recorded under her father's name. James M. Newman, Farm Book Three, 36 and 43, JMNPP.

17. After Ella Harris married Zee Ayers, Newman gave her a new account sheet. The unnumbered page says: 1 January to 27 June 1891 Ella Ayers work tasks.

18. Julia Ayers Anderson, interview, 12 July 1993.

19. Buckingham County Deed Book 9, 322.

20. Buckingham County Deed Book 11, 4 January 1902, 171.

21. Buckingham County Deed Book 13, 10 March 1905, 198.

22. Buckingham County Deed Book 15, 20 August 1910, 253, and Book 19, 5 April 1920, 276.

23. The two gifts of land that Ella Harris Ayers and Mandy Brown gave to George Ayers are recorded in the Buckingham County Tax Assessment Books for the years in which the actions took place.

24. During the interview Julia Ayers Anderson identified her grandfather to be a white man. When questioned further about his racial identity, Anderson responded that he looked just like a white man and that her parents always told her that he was a white man." He was not. Newman did not list Zee Ayers as a colored or "Yellow man" as he usually did when referring to mulattos. There were white and African American Ayers families listed in the population census as liv-

ing in the Belmont area. If Ella Harris married a white man, she is the only Belmont worker identified to have married outside of her race. Julia Ayers Anderson, interview by author, 12 July 1993. U.S. Bureau of the Census, Federal Census, Twelfth Population Schedule, 1900, Buckingham County, Va.

25. Most African Americans did what the Gregorys had done when they first purchased land in 1874. They went to the courthouse and let whites witness and record the land transactions. Starting in 1902, Zee Ayers took other blacks with him to have them sign. On 4 January 1902, Emma D. Gregory and S. L. Gregory witness his purchase. Buckingham County Deed Book 11, 171.

26. This house has not been occupied for many years. It is off Route 650 northeast of Dillwyn, Virginia. Two persons who lived in the house as children were identified by Julia Anderson, and one of them was interviewed. Mattie Pearl Swann Bethea described the floor and land layout as she remembered it. Mattie Pearl Swann Wade Bethea, interview, 25 October 1993.

27. Buckingham County Deed Book 9, 279.

28. James M. Newman, Farm Book Three, 33, JMNPP.

29. Ibid., William Gregory entries, 37.

30. Ibid., Samuel Gregory entries, 7. Sarah Woodson entries, 43. Quote taken from page 7.

31. Buckingham County Deed Book 10, 52.

32. Buckingham County Deed Book 12, 25.

33. Buckingham County Deed Book 14, 321. U.S. Bureau of the Census, Federal Census, Twelfth through Fourteenth Population Schedules, 1900–1920, Buckingham County, Va.

34. According to the 1910 census, Nannie Woodson was a widow, fifty-five years of age, who had given birth to eighteen children with only twelve of them living in that year. Woodson is also listed as unable to read and write and as living on rented farm property. In the 1880 census, Nannie Woodson had lived in a household headed by her husband Ben with six of their children, Robert, William, and Bennie among them. U.S. Bureau of the Census, Federal Census, Tenth through Thirteenth Population Schedules, 1800–1910, Buckingham County, Va.

35. U.S. Bureau of the Census, Federal Census, Ninth and Tenth Population Schedules, 1870 and 1880, Buckingham County, Va.

36. James M. Newman, Farm Book Three, 53, JMNPP.

37. Ibid.

38. Ibid., 54.

39. Ibid., entry for 25 November 1893.

40. U.S. Bureau of the Census, Federal Census, Thirteenth Population Schedule, 1910, Buckingham County, Va.

41. While this incident is not confirmed by written records, it is told consistently by the three oldest Van and Mary Woodson children. William Howard Woodson, 13 August 1993. Ethel Woodson Bolden, 15 October 1993. Wiley Gray Woodson, 25 November 1993.

42. Buckingham County Deed Book 21, 408.

43. Buckingham County Deed Book 21, 567.

44. Buckingham County Deed Book 22, 126. Listed along with Nannie Woodson as holders of the land are her sons Benny, John Wesley, and Alexander, and daughter Annie Woodson Forest.

45. James M. Newman, Farm Book Three, 128, JMNPP.

46. Ibid., 129.

47. Ibid., 130.

48. Ethel Woodson Bolden, interview, 15 October 1993.

49. U.S. Bureau of the Census, Federal Census, Twelfth and Thirteenth Population Schedules, 1900, 1910, Buckingham County, Va.

50. Buckingham County Deed Book 22, 89.

51. Edith Woodson Swann, interview, 4 July 1992.

52. U.S. Bureau of the Census, Federal Census, Ninth Population Schedule, 1870,

53. U.S. Bureau of the Census, Federal Census, Twelfth Population Schedule, 1900, Buckingham County, Va., entries for George Holman and Edward Shepherd.

54. U.S. Bureau of the Census, Federal Census, Thirteenth Population Schedule, 1910, Buckingham County, Va.

55. James M. Newman, Leather Pocket Notebook Three, JMNPP.

56. James M. Newman, Farm Book Two, JMNPP.

57. Buckingham County Deed Book 23, 89. U.S. Bureau of the Census, Federal Census, Thirteenth and Fourteenth Population Schedules, 1910 and 1920, Buckingham County, Va.

58. Buckingham County Judgment Lien Docket and Execution Book 3.

59. The account that Charles Swann "just walked off" is repeated by several members of the Swann family. There is no evidence of where he went. He never contacted his family again. Shirley Swann Brown, interview, 1 November 1993. Mattie Pearl Swann Bethea, interview, 25 October 1993.

4. Getting Things

1. These events occurred between 1865 and 1939. Polly Wade's death day is recalled in interviews with her grandnieces Ethel Woodson Bolden and Edith Woodson Swann. The man who dumped the peas onto the tablecloth was Lewis Morris, and this event took place on 29 October 1939, the wedding day of Edith Woodson and Linwood Swann. The farmer who loaded all of his daughter's things into a wagon was Alexander Morris. He did so on 9 October 1898. The unmarried freed woman with spasms was Judy Gregory; Newman recorded her pledge to earn a cure for herself in 1884. Ethel Woodson Bolden, interview, 3 March 1993. Edith Woodson Swann, interview, 13 March 1993. James M. Newman, Farm Book Three, 130, and Farm Book Two, 31, JMNPP.

2. U.S. Bureau of the Census, Federal Census, Eighth Population Schedule, 1860, Buckingham County, Va.

3. U.S. Bureau of the Census, Federal Census, Ninth Population Schedule, 1870, Buckingham County, Va.

4. John C. Page Estate Record, Cumberland County Court Will Book 12, 145.

5. Ibid.

6. William Shepard, "Buckingham Female Collegiate Institute," in *William and Mary Quarterly*, 2d ser., vol. 20 (1940), no. 2 (April): 167–193, and no. 3 (July): 345–368.

7. Ibid., no. 2, 192.

8. Ibid., no. 3, 363.

9. Roger L. Ransom and Richard Sutch, *One Kind of Freedom*, 6, 216–217.

10. Edward T. Page, Leather Pocket Notebook, ETPPP. See also James M. Newman, Farm Books, JMNPP.

11. Ransom and Sutch, *One Kind of Freedom*, 152.

12. Edward T. Page, Leather Pocket Notebook, ETPPP.

13. Ransom and Sutch, *One Kind of Freedom*, 152.

14. James M. Newman, Farm Book One, 36, JMNPP.

15. Edward T. Page, Leather Pocket Notebook, ETPPP.

16. Edward T. Page, Leather Pocket Notebook, ETPPP. U.S. Bureau of the Census, Federal Census, Ninth Agricultural and Production Schedule, 1870, Buckingham County, Va.

17. James M. Newman, Leather Pocket Notebook Two, JMNPP.

18. Ransom and Sutch, *One Kind of Freedom*, 5.

19. Edward T. Page, Leather Pocket Notebook, ETPPP.

20. Ransom and Sutch, *One Kind of Freedom*, 5.

21. Levi Pollard, for example, declared "everybody got winter clothes. . . . Every man gits two workin shirts, one coat, one pair pants, one jacket, en one pair shoes. De women git near bout the same I reckon." Charles L. Perdue, Jr., Thomas E. Barden, and Robert K. Phillips, *Weevils in the Wheat: Interviews with Virginia Ex-Slaves*, 229.

22. James M. Newman, Farm Books Two and Three, JMNPP.

23. Charles E. Orser, Jr., *The Material Basis of the Postbellum Tenant Plantation*, 57.

24. Ransom and Sutch, *One Kind of Freedom*, 6.

25. James M. Newman, Farm Book One, 18, JMNPP.

26. Edward T. Page, Leather Pocket Notebook, ETPPP.

27. Edward L. Ayers, *Promise of the New South*, 103.

28. U.S. Bureau of the Census, Federal Census, Third through Eighth Population Schedules, 1810–1860, Buckingham County, Va.

29. U.S. Bureau of the Census, Federal Census, Seventh Population Schedule, 1850, Buckingham County, Va.

30. Thomas J. Schlereth, "Country Stores, Country Fairs and Mail Order Catalogues: Consumption in Rural America," in Simon J. Bronner, *Consuming Visions*, 341.

31. Daniel Horowitz, "The Morality of Spending: Attitudes toward the Con-

sumer Society in America, 1875–1940," in Simon J. Bronner, *Consuming Visions,* 346–347.

32. Ibid. 352.
33. Ibid., 353–354.
34. Ibid., 363–369.
35. Sydney Nathans, "Gotta Mind to Move," 204–208; quote on 208.
36. Ibid., 216–217.
37. Joe A. Mobley, "In the Shadow of White Society," 340–384.
38. Ibid., 344–346.
39. Ibid., 340.
40. Ibid., 345–346.
41. Orser, Jr., *The Material Basis of the Postbellum Tenant Plantation,* 130.
42. Ibid., 122.
43. Ibid., 121.

5. Spoken Words

1. The granddaughter of slaves in this anecdote is Mary Wade Woodson (1888–1968). The old folks in Woodson's life would have been her mother-in-law Nannie Peaks, her uncle Wilson Morris, her parents Matt and Martha Wade, and grandfather Jerry Wade, all Caryswood and Belmont workers born before 1865. Her granddaughter, accustomed to duplicating her every action, is her third daughter Edith Woodson Swann's (1920–1995) third daughter, Georgia Swann Brown (1944–). Brown shared this story with her younger sister, the author, in May 1998 on the occasion of Swann-Wright's daughter's college graduation, when rain threatened to pour from the Blacksburg, Virginia, skies all morning and finally did so in the afternoon. Anecdotes and stories are often transmitted at life transition points such as births, marriages, graduations, and deaths. The transmission of this anecdote follows this classic pattern.

2. Paul Thompson, *The Voice of the Past: Oral History,* 139.

3. The grandmother in this anecdote is Juda Ann Monroe Swann (1852–1925). The now eighty-two-year-old woman is Swann's oldest son's second daughter, Mattie Pearl Swann Wade Bethea. The author grew up hearing this story. It was told numerous times, usually qualifying the experiences of early family members and thereby establishing family identity. Mattie Pearl Swann Wade Bethea, interview, 25 October 1993.

4. The exact year Charles Swann walked off and his final destination remain unknown. The 1910 census lists him as heading a household of five persons including his wife of thirty-two years, Juda Ann Swann, and three of their eleven children who were still living at home. The 1920 census shows both Charles and Juda Ann living in their oldest son's John Swann's household, with him and his wife Olivia Jane Swann and their four children. The last surviving child in the family remembers her grandmother coming to live at her childhood home after her grandfather had "just walked off forever." Shirley Swann Brown, the daugh-

ter of one of Charles Swann's younger sons, says that she was told that he went back to Africa, returning with hats which the family hung for years in the hallway of the family home. Bethea says that she never heard that story and knows that she never saw her grandfather again after he left and her grandmother came to live with her. Ibid.; Shirley Swann Brown, 1 November 1993.

5. J. Linwood Swann, the author's father, sang this song. Those who remembered the song included his sister, Mattie Pearl Swann Wade Bethea, wife Edith Woodson Swann, and brothers-in-law, William Howard Woodson and Wiley Gray Woodson. There are many reasons to believe that this was a song sung by Caryswood and Belmont workers. Swann's mother, Olivia Jane Tyree Swann (1888–1954) worked for Newman's neighbor and sister-in-law, Catherine Gannaway Trent. Perhaps her husband sang it to her during their courtship while she lived-in at the Trents as the 1900 census states that she did. J. Linwood Swann's maternal grandfather worked for Newman as did his maternal great-uncles Jacob, Esau, and Caesar Tyree, maternal great-grandfather Daniel Tyree, and paternal great-grandparents Charles and Juda Ann Swann. J. Linwood Swann grew up surrounded by these relatives and worked tobacco and corn fields with them. This song could well have been passed on to him by one of these men who had the privilege of deciding where his wife would work once freedom became a reality following the Civil War. For the role men played in determining the work places for women, see chapter 2, Work Relationships, and Jacqueline Jones, *Labor of Love, Labor of Sorrow*.

6. Charlotte Linde, *Life Stories: The Creation of Coherence*, 51–57.

7. Ibid.

8. See R. Baxter Miller, *Black Literature and Humanism*, 50.

9. Mattie Pearl Swann Wade Bethea, 25 October 1993.

10. Elizabeth Page Trent Bird, 29 September 1991; Edith Woodson Swann, 15 October 1993.

11. William Howard Woodson, Sr., 13 August 1993.

12. George Jordan Brown, 15 December 1995.

13. Ethel Woodson Bolden, 1 August 1993. William Howard Woodson tells this same story; his brother Wiley also knew about the pig, but said that it just "walked around the house sometimes," it did not actually live inside the house.

14. Bethea, 25 October 1993; Shirley Swann Brown, 1 November 1993.

15. Bethea, 25 October 1993.

16. Westa Winn Wood, 8 October 1998. Interviews with William Howard Woodson, 2 August 1993; Ethel Woodson Bolden, 4 July 1992; Wiley Gray Woodson, 25 November 1993; and Edith Woodson Swann, 15 October 1993.

17. Interviews with William Howard Woodson, Ethel Woodson Bolden, Wiley Gray Woodson, Edith Woodson Swann.

18. Edith Woodson Swann, 15 October 1993.

19. Ibid.

20. Ibid.

6. The End Result

1. Edward T. Page's gravestone reads:
Edward T. Page
SCA Army Regiment 14

2. James M. Newman Estate Records, Buckingham County Will Book 1, 531 and 524.

3. Newman made his final diary entry on 23 March 1900. The last words he wrote were: "I home busy-unwell." There were three full blank pages left in the volume. Newman had sewn pages together using a slip stitch to hold the pages together. James M. Newman, Farm Book Three, 150, JMNPP.

4. Newman agreed to sell Belmont to John and Stephen Trent for $1,250. Newman wrote in his diary that the farm totaled 265 acres (the deed was drawn on 9 January 1899). He also declared that he had purchased the farm for $3,200 "near 30 years before," which is untrue. Pattie Newman passed on full title to Belmont and "all of [her] furniture and any and all personal property" when she recorded her will on 4 November 1882. Pattie Newman died in July 1894. Her will was proved 8 October 1894 (five days after Newman's sixty-eighth birthday), making Newman the sole proprietor of Belmont. Buckingham County Will Book 1, 426 and 531. James M. Newman, Farm Book Three, 143. John and Stephen Trent, interview by the author, 14 March 1992.

5. See Wade, Morris, and Woodson family trees in Appendix.

6. The two black churches in this Buckingham-Cumberland County community dating to the 1870s are the Chief Cornerstone Church and the Baptist Union Church.

7. See photograph of Van and Mary Woodson with their children and extended family members at the beginning of this chapter.

8. While Lillian Wade Watkins was never officially acknowledged as Van Woodson's daughter, it was understood in the family that she was. Georgia Swann Brown shares that she remembers hearing Ethel Bolden call Lillian "my sister, my sister." Edith Swann has confirmed that "everyone knew that Lillian was Papa's. People just didn't talk about that back then." Georgia Swann Brown, 8 March 1993; Edith Woodson Swann, 27 November 1993.

9. William Howard Woodson tells this same story. For the full story, see "Dyin' Grace This Mornin" in chapter 5.

10. This story of Teen's death and the orange has been confirmed by each Woodson sibling interviewed.

11. For additional information concerning Ida Robinson, see E. Franklin Frazier, *The Negro Church in America*, 60–63. Frazier describes Robinson as "tall, sharp of feature and eye, medium brown in color, probably of mixed Indian-Negro blood."

12. Annie Wade had gone away to Philadelphia to find work. Her parents, Matt and Martha Wade, deeded the land for Bright Morning Star to its trustees in 1925.

13. This is a story I heard many times while growing up. Mr. John Swann was my father's father. The families of these two men were joined together when my parents married 31 October 1939, seven years after this incident occurred.

14. This story is told by the three oldest Woodson children. Sixty-one years after his father's death, Wiley Woodson still got tears in his eyes when he spoke of his father's death.

15. See family photo taken following Van Woodson's death in 1932 (chapter 5).

16. While many people suspected the truth, no one verbalized it. Marion Swann Carter, Edith's oldest daughter, and this writer's oldest sister, stated that "Sister" had told her the truth before she gave birth to her son. Marion Swann Carter, 27 November 1993.

17. Ethel Bolden has recounted this event many times and used it as the basis for her most moving sermons. She usually ends with the statement, "Now no body can't tell that my God ain't able!"

18. Ethel Bolden concluded her 15 October 1993 interview with this statement.

Bibliography

Primary Sources

Public Records

Buckingham County Birth and Death Records, 1869–1910. Buckingham County Courthouse, Buckingham, Va.

Buckingham County Deed Books 1–23. Buckingham County Courthouse, Buckingham, Va.

Buckingham County Judgment Lien Docket and Execution Books 1–3. Buckingham County Courthouse, Buckingham, Va.

Buckingham County Tax Assessment Book 3. Buckingham County Courthouse, Buckingham, Va.

Buckingham County Will Book 1. Buckingham County Courthouse, Buckingham, Va.

Cedar Baptist Church records, 1870–1900. Cedar Baptist Church Archive, Buckingham, Va.

Chief Cornerstone Baptist Church records, 1880–1930. Church records collection, in the care and possession of Mrs. Eliza Ann Spencer, church clerk. Mrs. Spencer resides in Buckingham County, Va.

Cumberland County Birth and Death Records, 1850–1910. Cumberland County Courthouse, Cumberland, Va.

Cumberland County Inventory and Appraisement Will Books 1–12. Cumberland County Courthouse, Cumberland, Va.

U.S. Bureau of the Census, Federal Census, Third through Fourteenth Population Schedules (1810–1920). Washington, D.C.: Government Printing Office.

U.S. Bureau of the Census, Federal Census, Ninth and Tenth Agricultural and Production Schedules (1870–1880). Washington, D.C.: Government Printing Office.

U.S. Department of the Interior, *Compendium of the Tenth Census* (1880), revised edition, Part I. Washington, D.C.: Government Printing Office, 1885.

Personal Papers

All of the following are part of the Caryswood Family Archive, Caryswood Farm, Dillwyn, Va.

Cary Family Papers.

Edward T. Page Personal Papers Collection (ETPPP). These include the following:
Half-Way Branch Account and Expense Book, 1854–1877
Leather Pocket Notebook, 1867–1877

James Moore Newman Personal Papers Collection (JMNPP). These include the following:

Evergreen Store Ledger and Journal, 1853–1867
Leather Pocket Notebook One, 1861–1867
Leather Pocket Notebook Two, 1866–1870
Leather Pocket Notebook Three, 1870s and 1880s
Leather Pocket Notebook Four, 1890s
Farm Book One (appears to cover late 1870s to mid 1880s)
Farm Book Two (appears to cover early 1880s to mid 1890s)
Farm Book Three, 1885–1900

Trent Family Papers.

ORAL HISTORY INTERVIEWS

Anderson, Julia Ayers. 12 July 1993, Dillwyn, Va. Interview notes.
Bethea, Mattie Pearl Swann Wade. 25 October 1993, Baltimore, Md. Interview notes.
Bird, Elizabeth Page Trent. 29 September 1991, Dillwyn, Va. Tape recording.
Bolden, Ethel Beulah Woodson. 4 July 1992, Harrisonburg, Va. Tape recording.
———. 3 March 1993, Dillwyn, Va. Interview notes.
———. 1 August, 15 October 1993, Dillwyn, Va. Tape recording.
Brown, George Jordan. 15 December 1995, Dillwyn, Va. Interview notes.
Brown, Georgia Swann. 8 March 1993, Dillwyn, Va. Interview notes.
Brown, Shirley Swann. 1 November 1993, Dillwyn, Va. Interview notes.
Carter, Marion Swann. 27 November 1993, Baltimore, Md. Interview notes.
Swann, Edith Woodson. 4 July 1992, Harrisonburg, Va. Tape recording.
———. 13 March, 15 October 1993, Dillwyn, Va. Interview notes.
———. 27 November 1993, Baltimore, Md. Interview notes.
Trent, John and Stephen. 14 March 1992, Dillwyn, Va. Interview notes.
Wood, Westa Winn. 8 October 1998, Charlottesville, Va. Interview notes.
Woodson, Wiley Gray. 25 November 1993, Baltimore, Md. Tape recording.
Woodson, William Howard. 2 August, 13 August 1993, Dillwyn, Va. Interview notes.

SECONDARY SOURCES

Antze, Paul, and Lambek, Michael. *Tense Past: Cultural Essays in Trauma and Memory.* New York, 1996.
Alderson, William T. "The Freeman's Bureau and Education in Virginia." *North Carolina Historical Review* 29, no. 1 (January 1952): 64–90.
Ayers, Edward L. *The Promise of the New South.* New York, 1992.
———, *Southern Crossings: A History of the American South, 1877–1906.* New York, 1995.
Ayers, Edward L., and John C. Willis. *The Edge of the South: Life in Nineteenth-Cen-*

tury Virginia. Charlottesville, Va., 1991.

Barron, Hal S. *Those Who Stayed Behind: Rural Society in Nineteenth-Century New England*. New York, 1984.

Bear, James A., ed. *Jefferson at Monticello*. Charlottesville, Va., 1967.

Bethel, Elizabeth R., *Promiseland: A Century of Life in a Negro Community*. Philadelphia, Pa., 1981.

Bitting, Samuel. *Rural Land Ownership among the Negroes in Virginia*. New York, 1915.

Blassingame, John W. "Using the Testimony of Ex-Slaves: Approaches and Problems." *The Journal of Southern History* 41, no. 4 (November 1975): 473–492.

Braden, Waldo. *The Oral Tradition in the South*. Baton Rouge, La., 1983.

Breen, T. H., and Stephen Innes. *Myne Owne Ground: Race and Freedom on Virginia's Eastern Shore, 1640–1676*. New York, 1982.

Brewer, James H. *The Confederate Negro*. Durham, N.C., 1969.

Bronner, Simon J., ed. *Consuming Visions. Accumulation and Display of Goods in America, 1880–1920*. New York, 1995.

Buni, Andrew. *The Negro in Virginia Politics, 1902–1965*. Charlottesville, Va., 1967.

Burdick, John. "From Virtue to Fitness." *Virginia Magazine of History and Biography* 93, no. 1 (1985): 14–35.

Clark, Thomas D. *Pills, Petticoats and Plows: The Southern Country Store*. New York, 1944.

Confino, Alon. "Collective Memory and Cultural History: Problems of Method." *American Historical Review* 102, no. 5 (December 1997): 1386–1403.

Cornelius, Janet Duitsman. *When I Can Read My Title Clear: Literacy, Slavery and Religion in the Antebellum South*. Columbia, S.C., 1991.

Dabney, Virginius. *Virginia: The New Dominion*. New York, 1971.

Daniel, Pete. "The Metamorphism of Slavery, 1865–1900." *Journal of American History* 66, no. 1 (1979): 88–99.

———. *Breaking the Land: The Transformation of Cotton, Tobacco, and Rice Culture since 1880*. Urbana, Ill., 1985.

Daniel, W. Harrison. "Virginia Baptist and the Negro, 1865–1902." *Virginia Magazine of History and Biography* 76

DuBois, W. E. B. "The Negroes of Farmville, Virginia: A Social Study." *United States Department of Labor Bulletin* No. 14, January 1898.

Eckenrode, H. J. *The Randolphs: The Story of a Virginia Family*. New York, 1946.

Engerman, Stanley L. "Black Fertility and Family Structure in the United States, 1880–1940." *Journal of Family History* 2 (Spring 1977): 117–138.

———. "Studying the Black Family." *Journal of Family History* 3 (Spring 1978): 78–101.

Foner, Eric. *Reconstruction: America's Unfinished Revolution*. New York, 1988.

Frazier, E. Franklin. *The Negro Church in America*. New York, 1974.

Gutman, Herbert. *The Black Family in Slavery and Freedom, 1750–1925*. New York, 1976.

Gwalthney, John L. *Drylongso: A Self Portrait of Black America*. New York, 1980.

Harrison, Fairfax. *The Virginia Carys.* New York, 1919.

Heatwolfe, Cornelius J. *A History of Education in Virginia.* New York, 1916.

Historic Buckingham, Inc. *The Geographic Center of Virginia: A Guide to Places and People in Buckingham County, Virginia.* Dillwyn, Va., 1981.

Hutton, Patrick H. *History as an Art of Memory.* Hanover, N.H., 1993.

Innes, Stephen. *Labor in a New Land.* Princeton, N.J., 1983.

Isaac, Rhys. *The Transformation of Virginia.* New York, 1988.

Jaynes, Gerald D. *Branches without Roots.* New York, 1986.

———. *Old South, New South: The Genesis of the Black Working Class in the American South.* New York, 1980.

Johnson, Clifton H. *God Struck Me Dead: Religious Conversion Experiences and Autobiographies of Ex-Slaves.* Boston, Mass., 1969.

Jones, Jacqueline. *Labor of Love, Labor of Sorrow: Black Women, Work, and the Family from Slavery to the Present.* New York, 1985.

Julien, Eileen. *African Novels and the Question of Orality.* Bloomington, Ind., 1992.

Kerr-Ritchie, Jeffrey R. *Freedpeople in the Tobacco South.* Chapel Hill, N.C., 1996.

Kidd, Randy, and Jeanne Stinson. *Virginia Historic Marriage Register: Lost Marriages of Buckingham County, Virginia.* Irvina, Ga., 1992.

Linde, Charlotte. *Life Stories: The Creation of Coherence.* New York, 1993.

Litwack, Leon F. *Trouble in Mind: Black Southerners in the Age of Jim Crow.* New York, 1998.

Logan, Rayford W. *The Betrayal of the Negro: From Rutherford B. Hayes to Woodrow Wilson.* New York, 1954.

Maloney, Eugene A. *A History of Buckingham County.* Dillwyn, Va., 1976.

Martin, J. D. *Today and Yesterday in the Heart of Virginia.* Farmville, Va., 1935.

Martin-Perdue, Nancy J., and Charles L. Perdue, Jr. *Talk about Trouble: A New Deal Portrait of Virginians in the Great Depression.* Chapel Hill, N.C., 1996.

Mellon, James, ed. *Bullwhip Days, The Slaves Remember: An Oral History.* New York, 1988.

Miller, R. Baxter, ed. *Black Literature and Humanism.* Lexington, Ky., 1981.

Mobley, Joe A. "In the Shadow of White Society: Princeville, A Black Town in North Carolina, 1865–1915." *North Carolina Historical Review* 63 (July 1986): 340–384.

Moger, Allen W. *Virginia: Bourbonism to Byrd, 1870–1925.* Charlottesville, Va., 1986.

Morgan, Lynda J. *Emancipation in Virginia's Tobacco Belt, 1850–1870.* Athens, Ga., 1992.

Nathans, Sydney. "Gotta Mind to Move, a Mind to Settle Down: Afro-Americans and the Plantation Frontier." In *A Master's Due: Essays in Honor of David Herbert Donald,* edited by William Cooper, Michael F. Holt, and John McCardell, 204–222. Baton Rouge, La., 1985.

Olson, David, and Nancy Torrance, eds. *Literacy and Orality.* Cambridge, 1991.

Orser, Charles E., Jr. *The Material Basis of the Postbellum Tenant Plantation: Historical Archaeology in the South Carolina Piedmont.* Athens, Ga., 1988.

Pennington, Margaret A., and Loma S. Scott. *The Courthouse Burned.* Waynesboro, Va., 1977.

Perdue, Charles S., Jr., Thomas E. Barden, and Robert K. Phillips. *Weevils in the Wheat: Interviews with Virginia Ex-Slaves.* Charlottesville, Va., 1976.

Ransom, Roger L., and Richard Sutch. *One Kind of Freedom.* Cambridge, Mass., 1977.

Robertson, James I. *Civil War Virginia: Battleground for a Nation.* Charlottesville, Va. 1970.

Roth, Michael S. *The Ironist's Cage: Memory, Trauma, and the Construction of History.* New York, 1995.

Russell, James. "Rural Economic Progress of the Negro in Virginia." *Journal of Negro History* 11 (October 1926): 549–567.

Rutman, Darrett B., and Anita H. Rutman. *A Place in Time: Middlesex County, Virginia, 1650–1750.* New York, 1984.

Schweninger, Loren. *Black Property Owners in the South, 1790–1915.* Chicago, 1990.

Shifflett, Crandall. *Patronage and Poverty in the Tobacco South.* Knoxville, Tenn., 1982.

Simpson, Josephus. "Are Colored People in Virginia in a Helpless Minority?" *Opportunity* 12 (December 1934): 373–375.

———, "The Best Negroes in the World." *Opportunity* 9 (September 1931): 283.

Thompson, Paul. *The Voice of the Past: Oral History.* New York, 1988.

Tosh, John. *The Pursuit of History: Aims, Methods and New Directions in the Study of Modern History.* New York, 1982.

Vandiver, Frank E. *Their Tattered Flags.* New York, 1970.

Virginia Magazine of Genealogy 28, no. 2 (May 1990): 87–95.

White, Charles. *The Hidden and the Forgotten.* Marceline, Mo., 1985.

Wiener, Jonathan. "Planter Persistence and Social Change." *Journal of Interdisciplinary History* 7, no. 2 (Autumn 1976): 235–260.

Williams, Rosa G. *Historical Inventory of Buckingham County.* Vol. 1, *A to L.* Richmond, Va., 1937.

Wolf, Eric R. *Europe and the People without History.* Los Angeles, 1997.

Woodson, Carter G. *The Rural Negro.* Washington, D.C., 1930.

Woodward, C. Vann. *The Burden of Southern History.* Baton Rouge, La., 1960.

Wright, Gavin. *Old South New South: Revolutions in the Southern Economy since the Civil War.* New York, 1986.

Index

Italicized page numbers refer to illustrations

Corbin, Letcher Bolden. *See* Wade, Letcher Bolden
corn, 40–41; husker, 37–38
corporal punishment, 14–15
Cottrel, Nannie Trent: family tree of, 157
courtship, 111
Creasy, Bell, 86–87
Cumberland County: demographics of, 9; formation of, 14. *See also* Union Hill
Cumberland County Courthouse, 59
Cunningham, Henry, 66
Curdsville District, 32–33, 169 nn. 2, 3
cures and homemade remedies, 40

death: stories about, 116–18, 121, 125–26, 172 n. 1, 175 n. 5
debt, 41; honoring of, 67; protection against, 61
Democratic Party, 18–19
Dillwyn, Va., 17, 19
Dolly (mare), 39, 48
Douglass, Frederick, 36
Du Bois, W. E. B., 167 n. 30
"Dyin' Grace This Mornin'" (traditional story), 116–18, 125–26

education: and African Americans, 17–18, 50, 136; in Buckingham County, 32–33; of women, 16
Edwards, Anne, of Surry, 148
Ellison, Ralph, 113
emancipation yard story, 112, 115
Evergreen, Va.: store at, 45, 159 n. 3

farm journals, 8–10, 33
farm newspapers, 37
Farmville, Va., 97
Farmville Mercury (Buckingham, Va., newspaper), 17
federal census (1870), 65, 78
federal census (1900), 85
federal census (1920), 87
folk culture, 74
Foner, Eric, 11–12
food: meat, 79, 94, 104, 105; rations, 54, 56–57, 167 n. 30; shortage of, 94, 125–26; stories about, 118–22

Ford, Etta, 153, 155
Ford, Sam, 75
Forest, Annie Woodson, 172 n. 44
Frank (blacksmith), 26
Frank (hired man at Evergreen), 45
Freedman's Bureau, 65
"Fried Chicken, a Few Peas, and Some Rolls" (traditional story), 121–22

Gannaway, John L., 16, 150, 165 n. 4
Gannaway, Judith Baker Lancaster Gilliam, 92, 165 n. 4, 166 n. 22
Gannaway, Pattie. *See* Newman, Pattie Gannaway (Mrs. James Moore)
Gannaway, Richard W., 93
Gannaway, Theodorick: children of, 165 n. 4; and the Civil War, 16; conveys Bell Branch, 31; family tree of, 150; founder of Cedar Baptist Church, 47; wealth of, 92, 93
Gannaway family: family tree of, 150
Garland, Elder, 47
Gibson & Watkins (merchants), 39
Gilliam, Emeline, 165 n. 4
Gilliam, William, 27, 45
Gospel Herald (newspaper), 38
grapes, 38
Gregory, Alexander, 80; as a farm day laborer at Belmont, 53–55, 78; working characteristics of, 67
Gregory, Eliza, 54
Gregory, Fanny Woodson: and the "Fried Chicken" story, 122
Gregory, George, 151, 153, 155
Gregory, Harriet, 54, 70–71, 78–80
Gregory, Henry, 51, 65, 78, 80
Gregory, James, 80
Gregory, John, 53–55, 65, 70–71, 78–80
Gregory, John, Jr., 78
Gregory, John, III, 80
Gregory, Judy, 54, 78, 96, 172 n. 1
Gregory, Kate, 54, 78, 96
Gregory, Martha, 63
Gregory, Sam, 78, 79–80
Gregory, Taylor, 78–79, 80
Gregory, William, 53, 78, 79, 80
guano, 38, 60
Gutman, Herbert, 73

The American South Series

Anne Goodwyn Jones and Susan V. Donaldson, editors
Haunted Bodies: Gender and Southern Texts

M. M. Manring
Slave in a Box: The Strange Career of Aunt Jemima

Stephen Cushman
Bloody Promenade: Reflections on a Civil War Battle

John C. Willis
Forgotten Time: The Yazoo-Mississippi Delta after the Civil War

Charlene M. Boyer Lewis
Ladies and Gentlemen on Display: Planter Society at the Virginia Springs, 1790–1860

Christopher Metress, editor
The Lynching of Emmett Till: A Documentary Narrative

Dianne Swann-Wright
A Way out of No Way: Claiming Family and Freedom in the New South